Buy or Sell
Real Estate After the
1997 Tax Act

Buy or Sell Real Estate After the 1997 Tax Act

A GUIDE FOR HOMEOWNERS AND INVESTORS

ROBERT IRWIN

John Wiley & Sons, Inc.

New York • Chichester • Weinheim • Brisbane • Singapore • Toronto

ISBN: 0-471-14723-0

Printed in the United States of America

10 9 8 7 6 5 4 3 2 1

Preface

—■—

The Taxpayer Relief Act of 1997 made historic changes to the tax code, especially in the area of real estate. If you are an investor in property, are planning on buying a home, or are a homeowner, these changes affect you.

The benefits can be enormous, in many cases amounting to tens of thousands of dollars in tax savings. Whether you're selling a commercial center or a single rental, you should end up paying significantly lower taxes on the gain from the sale. If you're selling your personal home, you may avoid paying any taxes at all on the gain from the sale (up to $500,000), and if that's the case, you won't have to worry about "rolling over" the money into another home — it becomes yours to spend as you will!

Needless to say, virtually everyone involved in real estate has been scrambling to learn the details of the new tax rules and how they will be affected. To that end, many accounting and legal firms have put out "quickie" books that give their interpretations of the new law.

The problem I have found with virtually all of these tomes is that they are universally hard, if not impossible, to read. The tax code itself is complex. And lawyers' interpretations too often tend not to simplify, but to make matters even more obtuse.

I'm not a lawyer or an accountant, but after spending 30 years in real estate, I know that I want simple answers that I can understand.

Therefore, virtually as soon as the new law was passed, I obtained a copy and pored over it. I also consulted with CPAs and others for their interpretations. I found the answers I wanted, and, along the way, felt that others might benefit from my observations. This book is the result. In it I share with you my opinions on how the new tax law affects buying and selling real estate.

A word of caution, however. While the new law that Congress passed rewrites many areas of the federal tax code, that code is also changed by other forces including correction bills, interpretations by the Internal Revenue Service (which generally enforces the tax code), and court rulings in cases brought by taxpayers. (In fact, this bill has so many confusing aspects that there may be more correction bills than normal.) Indeed, the tax code might more appropriately be thought of as a work in progress. It is continually being changed and reinterpreted.

As a result, the information presented in this book should not be thought of as chiseled in stone. It is, rather, informed opinion on the new rules at the time this was written. The reader is therefore cautioned to check with his or her tax professional before taking any action having tax consequences.

Contents

Buy or Sell
Real Estate After the
1997 Tax Act

SECTION I

Home Exclusion

CHAPTER ONE

Introduction

In 1997 Congress passed and President Clinton signed a sweeping tax reduction bill that was hailed as the most significant reform in 11 years, 21 years, or the century, depending on who was being quoted. Indeed, in some cases and for some individuals, the changes will be significant and will provide enormous tax cuts. On the other hand, the cuts will be relatively minor for others. And for a few there will actually be tax increases!

Some of the most significant tax changes in the bill affect real estate—a complicated capital gains reduction on property, a new up to $500,000 exclusion on the sale of a personal residence, and other reforms. In this book we will concentrate primarily on understanding these changes, seeing what effects they will have, and formulating strategies for taking the best advantage of them depending on your financial situation.

But first let's spend just a few moments on the concept of what a capital gains tax actually is.

What Is Capital and What
Is a Capital Gains Tax?

The United States taxes capital at a higher rate than virtually any other "advanced" nation, even after the current reduction. Other countries, particularly in Europe, have much higher taxes on income or spending, but not on capital. It's important to understand the difference.

The government has to raise money, and taxing income or spending seems a logical way to accomplish this in a capitalist society. It is a way to redistribute the wealth we produce and redirect it, through the federal and state governments, to mutually beneficial areas such as defense, education, transportation, and so on. (On the other hand, in a communist society, where the government theoretically provides all jobs, taxing income or spending would make little sense.)

At the most basic level, when we work we produce income, some of which is used to pay taxes and the remainder of which we can use to buy goods and services . . . or save. It's this savings that we need to concentrate on. Whatever income is not paid out in taxes or spent on goods and services—in other words, whatever income is saved—becomes capital. Capital is, in essence, the stored product of work. It is what's in our savings account and what we use to make a down payment on a house. In a larger sense it is what lenders use to give us a mortgage. In a much larger sense it is the engine used to finance corporations, which produce jobs, which in turn employ us. Without this essential capital, we couldn't buy houses. Indeed, there wouldn't even be apartments to rent.

Of course capital in the form of, say, gold sitting in a vault, would do no one any good. Capital must be used to fuel our economy. And most of us use capital all the time. If we are interested in low-risk capital investment, we typically buy bank CDs or Treasury bonds, and in return receive a small reward for our efforts.

On the other hand, if we are risk-takers we may invest our capital in start-up companies, hoping to get much higher rewards. It's these initially high-risk companies that provide the jobs that employ people in our society. Remember, at one time Intel, Microsoft, and others were just such high-risk ventures.

What's vital to understand is that risking capital is what makes our society work. If there were no capital or if people were not willing to risk it, there would be no corporations, no economic growth, no jobs, no building of wealth, and no simple way to buy and sell real estate.

Does It Make Sense to Tax Capital?

Remember, a tax on capital is a tax on saved income — income that has already been taxed once either as salary or as dividends.

Further, every time the government taxes capital, it reduces the amount of capital that is available to advance our society economically. If the rate of capital taxation is 20 percent, that means that of every dollar available to build a company, finance an apartment building, or develop a university, one-fifth has just been stolen away.

In short, taxing capital acts as a brake on economic growth. And the higher the capital gains tax rate, the bigger the brake. Tax capital at 100 percent and our society would quickly cease to function. Eliminate a tax on capital entirely and we would speed ahead, creating more jobs, more companies, and more homes, office buildings, and factories.

Therefore, while a reduction in the capital gains tax, such as we've seen, is to be applauded, it should be remembered that it is a small step. A significant harmful influence remains.

The truth of the matter is that we live in a capitalist society and taxing capital is anticapitalist. It's like the old saw about cutting off your nose to spite your face.

If the new tax law benefits you, enjoy your gain. But just remember how much greater that gain would be and how much more our society would benefit if the capital gains tax were entirely eliminated.

CHAPTER TWO

—❚—

The New Up to $500,000 Home Exclusion

WHEN PRESIDENT CLINTON, in the 1996 Presidential campaign, proposed an exclusion of up to $500,000 on the sale of a principal residence, enactment of such a law seemed a remote possibility. However, to the amazement of many, it was included in the final version of the 1997 Tax Reduction Act and may be available to you now. Let's consider just what this benefit actually is and whether you and your home do qualify.

It's important to understand the general consequences. Under the new up to $500,000 exclusion (The way the new rules are written, the exclusion is up to $250,000 per person—a married couple filing jointly, therefore, has a combined exclusion of up to $500,000), if you're an "empty nester," someone whose family has grown up and moved away, leaving you with a no-longer-necessary large home, you can probably downsize now without worrying about the tax consequences. Similarly, if you're been transferred by your company from an area of high-priced housing to one of low-priced housing, you can probably make the move without worrying that you'll have to pay tax on the changeover.

Indeed, the new rules make it far easier to choose the type of housing you want, whether it be high-priced, low-priced, or even rental! The reason is that you no longer have to fear the tax consequences of selling with a high capital gain.

Let's see how this actually works.

What Is an Exclusion?

An exclusion means that you don't have to pay taxes that would otherwise be due.

For example, when you sell your home, you may have a capital gain. The amount of your gain will depend on such things as how much you paid for the property, any improvements you added to it, and how much you sold it for. (We'll go into the actual calculation of a capital gain in a later chapter.) Let's say that you've owned the property for a number of years, prices have appreciated, and you have a capital gain of $100,000.

Normally, you would pay taxes on your gain at the appropriate rate. If the rate were 20 percent, you would owe $20,000 in taxes on the $100,000 gain. (Also check the next section to see how different rates of capital gains tax may apply.)

However, under the new exclusion rule, when a married couple sells a qualifying principal residence, up to $500,000 of the capital gain may be excluded. There's no tax to pay on it. In our example, since your gain is less than $500,000, your gain is fully excluded. In short, instead of owing $20,000 in taxes on your $100,000 gain, you owe nothing.

:: **HINT** ::

In order to get the full up to $500,000 exclusion for a married couple:

1. Both spouses must meet the usage test. (Must be the principal residence for the previous two out of five years)
2. Either spouse must meet the ownership test. (Only one need actually own the property.)
3. Neither may have sold (or exchanged) a residence within the previous two years.

EXAMPLE

You sell your home and realize a $235,000 capital gain. How much tax must you pay on the gain?

Answer: If you and the home otherwise qualify, no tax is due because the gain is under the maximum exclusion.

What Is the Amount of the Exclusion for Single People?

The law actually quantifies the exclusion at up to $250,000 per person. That's the amount of the exclusion for a single person or a married taxpayer filing separately. For a married couple, the amount is doubled—up to $500,000.

It doesn't matter how much your gain may be; the maximum amount you can exclude is determined by your marital status. If you're single and have a capital gain of $300,000 on the sale of a principal residence, then the first $250,000 would be excluded. However, you would have to pay tax on the remaining balance of the gain, or $50,000. The amount of tax you would pay would of course be determined by a variety of factors (again, see the next section).

EXAMPLE

The exclusion for married couples filing jointly is up to $500,000.

The exclusion for singles or married individuals filing separately is up to $250,000.

(We'll have more to say about special circumstances shortly.)

Why Do You Keep Saying the Amount Is UP to $500,000?

Although it may seem self-evident to some, it's probably worthwhile to point out for those new to exclusions that they do not work like tax credits. If your gain is less than the maximum, you lose the remainder of the exclusion.

For example, let's say you're married filing a joint return and your capital gain is $150,000. Since you're well within the maximum limitation, you exclude the full amount. But, you may ask, what about the remaining $350,000 of the $500,000 exclusion? Who gets that?

If this is something you are pondering, think of it this way. You take your daughter shopping and tell her that she should buy herself a gift with up to $5.00 of her own money and you'll pay her back for whatever she spends, up to the maximum of $5.00. She goes out and spends $1.50 (a very frugal child indeed!). Now, how much do you owe her?

Obviously, you owe her $1.50. But she gets upset and says you told her you'd pay up to $5.00. Where's the other $3.50? She wants it, and right now!

Are you going to pay her the additional $3.50 for money she didn't spend? Not if you want to teach her the value of money. Is the government going to let you use any part of the $500,000 exclusion you don't qualify for? Not in a million years.

EXAMPLE

You are married and sell your qualifying principal residence, realizing a capital gain of $27,000. What is your tax advantage?

If you qualify, you do not have to pay any tax on the $27,000. However, you get no benefit whatsoever from the remaining $473,000 of the exclusion.

What Can I Do with the Capital Gain from My House That I Now Don't Have to Pay Tax On?

You can do what you want with the money—invest it in a new house, buy a car, put it in the bank, take a vacation, blow it in Las Vegas. The money is yours, tax free, to do with as you wish. You will, however, have to indicate on your tax return for the year that you indeed sold your principal residence, received a gain, and excluded that money.

Is it really that simple?!

It really is—almost. The real issue becomes, Do you and your house qualify for the exclusion? In this and the next chapter, we'll consider some of the necessary qualifications.

Is It Your Principal Residence?

This can be confusing for many people. We are talking here *only* about your principal residence. This is not to be confused with residential property. (*Residential* simply means any property, from single-family dwellings to apartment buildings to condos and co-ops, where people live or "reside.")

You can only have one principal residence at a time. This is important and must be remembered. If you have two homes (for example, a regular and a vacation home), only one at a time can be your principal residence.

Which one is your principle residence is largely determined by where you spend most of your time. Evidence of a home being your principal residence might include such things as having your mail delivered there, having utilities and phone service to the home in your name, working in the area, or voting in the area. But, of course, the final consideration is that you must actually live there most of the time.

A Principal Residence Can Take Many Forms

It can be a single-family house, one-half of a two-unit "duplex," one unit of a four-unit "four-plex," a mobile home, a houseboat, or even recreational vehicle (RV) such as a large motor home. The important thing is that you own it (not rent it) and that you live there most of the time. Note: in the case of a dwelling that is part principal residence and part not (for example, a duplex), the part in which you live is considered your principal residence and the other part (which you presumably rent out) is considered investment property. On sale, the part that qualifies as a principal residence would be subject to the exclusion, while the nonqualifying part would be subject to tax on any capital gain.

:: :: ::
EXAMPLE

You have lived in a "triplex," three identical residential units in a single building on a single lot, for the past three years. You occupy one-third of the building and rent the remaining two-thirds out. You sell the building, realizing a capital gain of $300,000. Do you owe any taxes?

Answer: Assuming each unit has the same fair market value, because one-third of the building was your principal residence, one-third of the capital gain up to $500,000 (for married couples filing jointly) is excluded from being taxed. You owe no taxes on $100,000. However, because two-thirds of the building was investment real estate, you owe capital gains tax on the balance of the gain—$200,000.

:: :: ::

> ## ⁕ HINT ⁕
>
> Some readers may be wondering what happens if
> the state condemns a taxpayer's principal residence
> to put a road through. That is considered an invol-
> untary conversion, and as far as the exclusion is con-
> cerned, all involuntary conversions, whether caused
> by condemnation, theft, seizure, requisition, or
> destruction, are treated as sales. It is not clear, how-
> ever, what effect, if any, the involuntary conversion
> has on the two out of five year rule.

You Must Have Lived in It for Two out of the Past Five Years

It is not enough that you simply own and live in the subject
property. You must have lived in it for any two of the previous five years. Note: we're not simply saying that you owned
it and rented it out, or owned it as a second home but did not
live there; you must have actually made the property your
principal residence for two of the previous five years.

The years do not have to be consecutive. You may have
bought a property, lived in it for six months, moved out and
rented it for two years, moved back in for a year and a half,
and then moved out and rented it again for a year. If, during
all of that time, you actually lived in the property for two out
of the previous five years, you qualify.

> ## ⠶ EXCEPTION ⠶
> If you become either mentally or physically incapac-
> itated (incapable of caring for yourself) and must
> live in a nursing home (a licensed care facility), the
> time you must have lived in your principal residence
> to get the exclusion is reduced to *one* year out of the
> previous five.

Dates are important here. You might miss the cutoff, and
the exclusion, by as little as one day if you're not careful. For
example, consider the following scenario. John and Janet
bought their home on January 1 for $100,000 and lived in it
for two years. At the end of that time, they moved and rented
the home out. They began renting it on July 1. Consequently,
as of that date it stopped being their principal residence.

Timeline

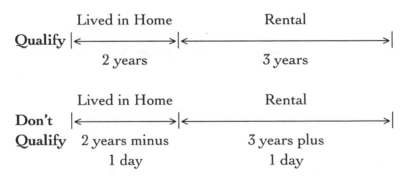

John and Janet rented the property for two years and
nine months, then decided to sell it. Naturally, they wanted
to take advantage of the exclusion. They immediately put the
home up for sale. How much time do they have to sell it
before the limitation on the two out of five years runs out?

If they sell it instantly, then it was a rental for only two years and nine months and they lived in it at least two years prior to that, meeting the two out of five year requirement. On the other hand, assuming that the property continued to be a rental during the selling period, what if it didn't sell until July 1?

Three years of rental ended on June 30; July 1 made three years and one day as a rental. Therefore, it would have been impossible for John and Janet to have lived in the property as a principal residence for two out of the previous five years. They would lose the exclusion and would have to pay tax on any capital gain they realized.

That could be a real financial blow for John and Janet. Assume that during the roughly five-year period, homes had skyrocketed in value and the couple had a capital gain of $50,000. If they could take the exclusion, they would, of course, have no tax to pay. If, on the other hand, they could not take the exclusion, they would need to pay tax on the $50,000. If we assume a 20 percent capital gains rate, John and Janet would have had to pay $10,000 in taxes. All because of one day!

Remembering dates is vital if you want to take full advantage of the new exclusion.

_____ ▉ ▉ ▉ _____

EXAMPLE

You owned a house for three years, using it as a principal residence for one and renting it out for two. You do not qualify.

You owned a house for three years, using it as a principal residence for two years and renting it out for one year. You do qualify.

You owned a house for five years and at different times (not continuously) lived in it as a principal residence for 24 months. You do qualify.

———————————————— ▪▪ ▪▪ ▪▪ ————————————————

What if They Moved Back In?

One final observation on our example is important. John and Janet could have rendered the entire issue of dates moot simply by moving back into the property and using it as their principal residence during the selling period. Remember, they rented it out for two years and nine months before deciding to sell. If they could have gotten their tenants out at that point (assuming the tenants were not on a long-term lease) and moved in themselves, the qualifying problem would be moot. (This is a good reason for planning for the long term when you give tenants a lease.)

Remember, as long as you don't rent the property out for more than three out of the previous five years, and if you move back in, reestablishing the property as your principal residence, you qualify for the exclusion.

When Does the New Law Take Effect?

The effective date of the new law was May 7, 1997, the date the budget deal (of which the $500,000 exclusion was a part) was agreed on. If your principal residence sold on or after May 7, 1997 (or if you had a legitimate binding sales agreement by that date but had not yet closed), then the new rules apply to you.

However, if you sold your home (closed escrow) prior to that date, then the old rules apply. We'll discuss those old rules and some exceptions to the dates in the next chapter.

CHAPTER THREE

Using the Up to $500,000 Home Exclusion

Y OU NOW KNOW what the up to $500,000 exclusion is (see the last chapter) and some basics on qualifying for it. Now, however, we're going to expand our discussion and talk about some of the other qualifying requirements of this new law and additional ways to take advantage of it.

How Often Can I Use the Exclusion?

You can only use it once every two years. If you buy and then resell a principal residence in less than two years, your capital gain (if any) will be subject to tax. (There is an exception here, which we'll discuss shortly.)

This two-year rule actually favors people who change homes frequently. Indeed, those who buy fixer-uppers, live in the properties for a few years while refurbishing them, and then sell are perhaps the biggest winners.

Of course, whether you fix up a home or not, you can change homes every two years, providing you have lived in the home during that time (it's your principal residence), and claim up to a $500,000 exclusion on your capital gain each time.

Of course, you would need to have the wisdom of Solomon to pick only those houses that rapidly increase in value! However, if you bought expensive homes in rapidly appreciating areas, you could potentially exclude $50,000, $100,000, $200,000—up to $500,000 (for marrieds filing jointly) every two years. Suddenly house-hopping could become a very profitable endeavor for ambitious people!

EXAMPLE

You've lived in your principal residence for 18 months and sell it; can you get the full exclusion?

No, you must have lived in it for a minimum of two years. (But you may get a partial exclusion—read on!)

You've lived in your principal residence for 22 months when you enter into a sales agreement. However, you do not close escrow until 24 months and one day after you bought the property. Do you qualify?

Yes, because you owned the property for more than two years.

Caution

One of the recurring themes of this book is that the tax laws are in a constant state of flux. What is true today may change tomorrow. As we'll see later in this chapter, some people who relied on the old tax laws are coming up big losers. The rule to remember is: Don't bet your future on today's tax laws. Tomorrow the qualification could change to three out of five years or the maximum exclusion could be reduced to $100,000 . . . or raised to $1 million.

What if I Have a Mandatory Job Change?

If a change in location of your employment, or a health condition or other unforeseen circumstance, demands that you sell your principal residence before the mandatory two-year requirement, you can still get some of the exclusion. The amount you get is based on the amount of time you already lived in the property. For example, if you are forced to sell, as noted previously, after only one year and you're married, you would qualify for half the maximum $500,000 exclusion. If you were a single person forced to sell after six months, you would qualify for one-fourth of the $250,000 maximum exclusion for single persons, or $62,500.

⁑ HINT ⁑

The IRS can be expected to establish strict rules for determining what would be an unforeseen circumstance that could force you to sell the property within less than two years. If you do sell in less than two years and there are no unforeseen circumstances, then the general rules on capital gains outlined in the next section would apply.

The actual amount of the exclusion that you would get in a qualifying sale of less than two years is determined by a formula based on the number of qualifying months divided by 24 months times the maximum exclusion.

$$\frac{\text{Qualifying months}}{24 \text{ months}} \times \$500,000 \ (\$250,000 \text{ for singles})$$

⁑ HINT ⁑

The tax code is not clear on the actual formula to be used for determining the amount of the exclusion in a qualifying sale of less than two years. While the text as well as the committee reports suggest that the formula just given is appropriate for determining this exclusion, some accountants have suggested that the actual formula should be quite different.

The alternate formula is as follows:

$$\frac{\text{Qualifying months}}{24 \text{ months}} \times \text{Capital gain}$$

The difference between the two interpretations is enormous. Be sure to check with your accountant for his or her interpretation before taking any action on the matter.

Just remember that you can't just decide to sell in less than two years. The matter has to be beyond your control and determined by employment, health, or other unforeseen circumstances. It remains to be seen how strictly the Internal Revenue Service will interpret this aspect of the new law; judging by past similar rules, however, it will probably be quite rigid.

⁑ HINT ⁑

If you move prior to the two-year holding period and the reason for the move is not a circumstance beyond your control—in other words, you choose to move—then you will not have the benefit of the exclusion on any gain.

For taxpayers this would amount to a significantly higher rate. Gains on residences held less than 18 months and not sold because of unforeseen circumstances would be taxed at a significantly higher rate (the midterm capital gains rate). Properties held between 18 months and two years should qualify for the lowest capital gains tax treatment. Gain on property sold in less than 12 months will be taxed at ordinary rates.

:: HINT ::

Although there is some confusion surrounding it, a provision of the new rules may be that if you owned the property on the day the bill was enacted (August 5, 1997) and sell it within two years after that day, you might not have to meet the two-year use and residence requirement. Check with your accountant.

How Many Times in Five Years Can I Claim the Exclusion?

In theory, you could claim it up to three times, at least in the first five years. Consider the following: you're married and have been living in a house for several years (more than two) and now you sell. Since this is your first sale in more than two years, the two-year rule begins to run.

Using a simultaneous escrow, you buy another principal residence on the same date as you sell your old one. You live in it two years and sell. And you do it again.

If you add up all the sales, you find that you have sold three homes in a period of less than five years, beginning with the first sale, and qualify for an exclusion of up to $500,000 on each home. Of course, from now on you must wait for two years each time.

What Happened to the Old Once-in-a-Lifetime $125,000 Exclusion?

Prior to enactment of the new up to $500,000 exclusion, people who reached the age of 55 could, once in their lifetimes, take an exclusion of up to $125,000 on the capital gain realized from the sale of a principal residence. The old rule had a number of qualifications, the most important of which was that in addition to being at least 55 years old, you had to have lived in the property for *three* of the previous of five years.

This old rule is superseded by the new rule. Be sure you understand that there is no longer any age requirement. You don't have to be at least 55 years old to take advantage of the new rule. You could be 54 or 24 or 67. Age is no longer a qualifying consideration. Further, while the old rule was *three* out of five years, the new rule is *two* out of five years. You've gained an extra year to play with.

What if I Already Took the Once-in-a-Lifetime Exclusion?

Congratulations! You've learned how to get the most from Uncle Sam. Under the old rules, once you took the $125,000, you (and your spouse) were prohibited from taking it again. It was a once-in-a-lifetime provision.

Under the new rule, however, having already taken the old $125,000 exclusion in no way precludes you from taking up to $500,000 (for marrieds filing jointly) each time you sell future principal residences (provided, of course, you've lived in them for the previous two out of five years).

Remember, the old rule was a once-in-a-lifetime rule. The new exclusion is an every-two-years rule. The new rule supersedes the old. It's one of those rare situations where you can have your cake and eat it too!

⚏ ⚏ ⚏

EXAMPLE

I'm 57 years old and married filing jointly. Two years ago, when I was 55, I sold my principal residence and took the once-in-a-lifetime $125,000 exclusion. I immediately bought another home and now want to sell it. Can I claim the up to $500,000 exclusion?

Answer: Yes. Having taken the old $125,000 exclusion in no way precludes your taking the new up to $500,000 exclusion. You've lived in your principal residence for the mandatory two years.

⚏ ⚏ ⚏

What Happened to the "Rollover" Rule?

The old rule regarding the sale of a principal residence was that you could defer the gain on the sale by "rolling it over" into a new residence once every two years. This meant that you had to purchase and occupy your new home within two years before or after the sale of your old one to qualify. Further, to fully defer all of the capital gain, the price of the new home had to be higher than the selling price of the old one. (If the new home cost less, then only a portion of the capital gain could be deferred.)

Note that the old rule was not an exclusion but a deferral. It's important to understand the difference.

Under the old rule, nothing was given to you. You still owed tax on any capital gain you might have on the sale of your property. What you got was the ability to defer paying that tax into the future. (As we'll see shortly, if you were clever and lucky, you could defer it so far into the future that it never got paid!)

For example, a couple might have bought a home 30 years ago for $25,000. They later rolled that over into a $60,000 home, then another costing $200,000, and yet another at $500,000. Over the years they bought ever more expensive homes, yet owed no tax because each time the gain was rolled over into the next house.

Of course, at retirement time such couples were often stuck with very expensive homes. That was the reason that the old once-in-a-lifetime $125,000 exclusion was originally enacted: to allow older people (those over 55) to downsize to a smaller home. (Of course, you might just never sell that last home and instead keep it until you died, at which time your spouse or heirs would get it at a "stepped-up" basis—its value at the time. In short, if you died while still living in that rolled-over principal residence, the deferred tax might never get paid!)

As a matter of fact, for sales enacted after the effective date of the new law, the old rollover rule no longer exists.

∷ HINT ∷

Another area of confusion relates to a home you bought and into which you rolled over gain from the sale of another residence under the old deferral rules. It appears that the periods of use and ownership of your prior rolled-over residences might be used in determining the use and ownership of the current residence for purposes of claiming the exclusion. Again, check with your accountant.

Those with Capital Gains of More than $500,000 Are Big Losers

The big losers in the new tax law are the super-wealthy and those, often in the middle class, who have rolled homes over for a long time.

If you bought a home for $1.5 million and saw it appreciate to $2.5 million, when you sell you suddenly have a big tax to pay. You have a $1 million capital gain. You can exclude the first $500,000 (assuming you're married and otherwise qualify), but you'll pay capital gains tax on the balance of $500,000. At a 20 percent rate, that's a whopping $100,000 in taxes! Under the old rules, you could roll that capital gain over into a more expensive home. Not anymore, however. Now there is no rollover rule—you must pay the tax on any capital gain that is not excluded.

Of course, when we talk about owners of super-expensive homes, we're not talking about a great many people. In California, the state with the greatest number of real estate sales, only about 3000 homes a year are sold for more than $1 million. Nevertheless, if you happen to be in that enviable category, you could take a big tax hit. (One of the reasons that an exclusion of $500,000 was so politically popular was that the vast majority of Americans could never take advantage of more than about $50,000 in gain. The big numbers sounded impressive, yet resulted in little actual loss of tax dollars for the Treasury.)

Some middle-class taxpayers, however, can also be losers. Remember our earlier example of the couple who bought a home for $25,000, rolled it over into a home for $60,000, then another for $200,000, and yet another for $500,000? What if they ended up owning a house worth $850,000, almost all of that in the form of deferred capital gain? Now when they sell, even after they take the $500,000 exclusion, they will have a big capital gain on which they will have to pay tax.

You don't need to be super-rich to lose here. You only need to have rolled your home over and over for a long period of time, to have never refinanced, and to have been lucky enough to see your property values go up.

▦ ▦ ▦

EXAMPLE

I'm married filing jointly, and I sold my house, where I had lived for the past five years, for $1.7 million. I had a capital gain of $700,000, of which $400,000 was appreciation on the sale of the home and $300,000 was deferred capital gain rolled over from previous homes. Do I owe any capital gains tax?

Answer: Yes, you do. You have a capital gain of $700,000. The first $500,000 is excluded. You owe capital gains tax on the remaining $200,000. The fact that a portion of the gain was previously deferred is irrelevant here.

▦ ▦ ▦

What if You Sold Your House Prior to May 6, 1997?

The new rules took effect on that date. However, if you sold your principal residence prior to that date, then the old rollover rules still apply to you. You cannot claim the up to $500,000 exclusion. But, you have two years within which to roll your capital gain over into a new home.

In addition, if you closed prior to May 6, 1997, you also should take advantage of the old once-in-a-lifetime $125,000 exclusion, providing you otherwise qualify.

▦ ▦ ▦

EXAMPLE

I'm married filing jointly, and I sold my house on May 5, 1997. Do I get an exclusion?

Answer: If you were 55 years of age and otherwise qualified under the old exclusion rules, you could take an exclusion of up to $125,000. If not, you could buy another home within two years for at least as much as the old and roll your entire capital gain into that new home (assuming you qualified under the old rollover rules). When you sold your new home, provided you kept it as a principal residence for two years, you would then qualify for the up to $500,000 exclusion on any capital gain.

※ ※ ※

What if I Sold My House after May 6 but before August 5?

While the new rules were postdated to take effect when the budget deal was originally reached, Congress did not pass the law and the President did not sign it into effect until August 5, 1997. For those who either sold their homes or had a legitimate sales contract between those two dates or who purchased a new home during that time, there may be some latitude.

Although a definitive answer has not been given as of this writing, there is some possibility that those in between, as just described, may be able to take advantage of either the old or the new rules. This means that if you are in a high-priced area, you may still be able to use the old rollover rule.

Further, if during the two years prior to August 5 (or maybe May 7) you purchased a qualifying new home but did not yet sell your old home, you may have as long as two years to sell the old home under the old rules. Remember, under the rollover rules you had up to two years before or after the purchase of a new home to roll over the old one.

Be sure to check with your accountant for more information on these possibilities.

:: **EFFECTIVE DATES** ::

The new exclusion, as well as the repeal of the old rollover rules and the once-in-a-lifetime $125,000 exclusion, apply to the sale (or exchange) of a principal residence after May 6, 1997.

However, you may choose to apply the previous rules, provided you otherwise qualify and

1. The sale (or exchange) was made prior to August 5, 1997.
2. You had a binding contract for sale by August 5, 1997 and the sale was later completed.
3. You acquired the replacement home prior to August 5, 1997.

What if I Sell for a Capital Loss?

The recent real estate recession (between approximately 1990 and 1996) produced many losers. Many people have yet to see their property values return to their former levels. Those who bought at the height of the market (the late 1980s/early 1990s) may actually have a capital loss when it comes time to sell.

Unfortunately, there has been no change in the rules here. As in the past, while a capital gain is taxable, a capital loss on the sale of a personal residence is not. If this is something new to you, be sure you understand it clearly. When you sell your personal residence (just as when you sell a vacation home, RV, boat, plane, or other similar property) *for a loss*, there is no tax relief available. You may not deduct that loss from your income.

:: HINT ::

It is the nature of the property at the time of sale that governs loss deductions. For example, if you had previously used the property as a principal residence, but then rented it out and subsequently sold it for a loss, you might be able to claim that loss against your ordinary income (up to the limits allowed annually). At the time of the loss, it would not be a personal residence but an investment property.

:: :: ::

EXAMPLE

I bought my home for $175,000 in 1990 and recently sold it for $145,000. I have a $30,000 capital loss. Can I deduct this from my income taxes?

Answer: No. Capital losses on principal residences remain nondeductible.

:: :: ::

If you are a homeowner facing a capital loss, however, this does not mean that your situation is hopeless. You may want to convert the property to a rental (as described above). A capital loss deduction is available on investment property; however, net capital losses are limited to $3000 per year. Further, a capital loss on one piece of investment property may be offset by a capital gain on another piece of investment property. If you have other investment real estate you are planning to sell in the future for a gain, you may be able to use a capital loss to lower your taxes there.

The issue is, For how long must you convert to a rental before a property changes from being categorized as a principal residence to an investment? This is a gray area, and some accountants like to figure on a two-year minimum period. However, as soon as you convert your home to a rental, you must begin claiming depreciation, something only available on investment property. For this reason other accountants feel that the transition period is virtually instantaneous. Check with your accountant.

CHAPTER FOUR

——❖——

Downsizing and Other Opportunities

T HE NEW HOME exclusion indirectly provides a variety of benefits to different members of society. There are benefits for seniors and for divorcees as well as some pitfalls to watch out for. In this chapter we'll consider some pluses and minuses of the new law.

What Are the Specific Downsizing Benefits?

In the past, as noted in earlier chapters, the only tax relief for a senior who wanted to sell a large home and acquire a smaller property was the old once-in-a-lifetime $125,000 exclusion. The problem with that rule, however, was that over the years, rolling over several homes, many seniors had acquired a greater amount of capital gain than they could exclude.

Further, in some cases couples had taken the $125,000 exclusion earlier. Since it was available once only, these people could not benefit from it later in life when they might need to downsize a second time.

A senior living alone after a spouse died might have no use for a full-size home, but instead might like to downsize to a duplex, a condo, or even an apartment. However, if the couple had already taken the $125,000 exclusion in prior years, it would no longer be available. On sale, all of the capital gain would be taxed. The result would be that often a senior would choose not to sell, instead living in an unsuitable home. Or, if the property was sold, the seller would have to give up a sizable portion of the gain—money needed for retirement—in taxes.

EXAMPLE

A senior couple wants to downsize to a duplex, a condo, or an apartment. However, over the years they have rolled properties over several times and their capital gain is $300,000. In the past, their exclusion would be only $125,000, meaning that they would still owe significant tax on the remaining capital gain. As described, they might choose to remain in an unsuitable dwelling rather the give up the money in taxes.

The new exclusion rules solve these problems in two ways. First, the exclusion has been increased significantly. The rules basically state that each individual may exclude up to $250,000. Thus, for a surviving senior, there is a significant exclusion available. A couple may take up to $250,000 each, or $500,000 total, so the exclusion will cover the vast majority of all seniors.

Second, the exclusion may be taken repeatedly. If the couple (or single) took an exclusion years before, it is permissible to take it again.

■ ■ ■

EXAMPLE

A senior husband and wife sold their large home 10 years ago and moved into a small townhouse. They took the $125,000 exclusion at the time. Since then one spouse has died and now the surviving senior needs to sell the townhouse and use the funds realized to help pay for care in a nursing home. Under the new rules, the senior can sell, claim an exclusion of up to $250,000, and feel free to use the money as necessary without having to worry about losing a significant portion of it to taxes.

■ ■ ■

Thus, a senior who wishes to downsize a second time in his or her later years and use the money for nursing home care benefits from the new tax law.

■ HINT ■

Your qualifying period of ownership includes the time your spouse, now deceased, also owned the residence.

Are There Benefits to Divorcees?

In the past, one of the important bones of contention in a divorce was who got the house. One reason this was significant from a tax perspective was because the spouse with the home was the one who could claim it as a principal residence, roll it over into another home, and, if a senior, claim the up to $125,000 exclusion. The other spouse was, so to speak, up the river without a paddle, often having to pay taxes on gain received from the sale.

Under the new law, however, each spouse is entitled to a $250,000 exclusion. If one spouse has the home and then sells it, as long as it was the principal residence of the other spouse for any two of the previous five years, both spouses can claim the exclusion.

EXAMPLE

After five years of marriage and living in one home, Ted and Alice divorced and Ted got their home as part of the settlement. Two and a half years later, Ted sold the property, and as a result of that sale Ted and Alice each received $65,000 in capital gain. Do either Ted or Alice owe tax on the money?

Answer: Because the home was their principal residence for at least two of the previous five years, each can claim up to $250,000 in exclusion. Ted had lived in the property continuously. Alice, however, had not lived in the property for two and a half years. Nevertheless, she still fulfilled the two out of five year rule and qualified.

EXAMPLE

John and Mary divorced and Mary got their home as part of the settlement. She lived in the home for four years and then sold. As part of the sale John and Mary each received $140,000 in capital gain. Do either owe tax on the money?

Answer: Mary owes no tax on her portion because she qualified for the up to $250,000 exclusion for individuals by using the home as her principal residence for at least two of the previous five years. However, John may not similarly qualify.

#

 # HINT #

During a divorce, if a home is *transferred to you* as part of the divorce proceedings, and if your spouse (or former spouse) resides in that home under the terms of a separation or divorce proceeding, the home is presumed to be your principal residence during that time frame.

What about State Capital Gains Laws?

One of the forgotten areas of the new tax law has to do with state coordination. In the past, virtually all states had capital gains laws and principal residence exclusions that matched the federal laws. Thus, for example, if you could roll your home over according to the federal rules, generally you could do likewise as part of the state rules. If you could take a federal once-in-a-lifetime up to $125,000 exclusion, you could take a similar state benefit.

However, the fact that the federal government has passed a new capital gains tax law in no way automatically changes state laws. It is now incumbent on each individual state to change its laws to coordinate with federal law if it so chooses. Thus, we may have a situation, at least temporarily, in which you will get the up to $500,000 exclusion at the federal level, but may be subject to the old rollover and up to $125,000 exclusion at the state level.

EXAMPLE

On September 15, 1997, you sell your home and realize a $350,000 capital gain. You are married and have used the property as your main home for at least two out of the previous five years, so you claim the federal exclusion. As a result, you pay no taxes at the federal level.

However, your state legislature is divided and does not pass laws coordinating the state rules to the federal ones. It continues to use the old rules. You now have two years in which to rollover the gain for state tax purposes. If you do not roll it over into a new property, you may have to pay state tax on your capital gain.

EXAMPLE

You are over 65 and you lived in your home for five years, then rented it out for the next three years before selling it (you are over 55 at the time of sale). At the federal level you can take advantage of the new exclusion rules.

Your state, however, has not adopted coordinating rules and instead uses the old rollover rules. Since you did not live in the home for the previous three years, you may not be able to claim it as a principal residence under the old state rules. You may owe state tax on your capital gain at the time of sale. Further, you may not be able to claim the old state once-in-a-lifetime up to $125,000 exclusion.

:: :: ::

States that do not adopt tax rules that mirror the federal rules put their citizens in a difficult situation. It is anticipated the eventually all states will adopt coordinating rules. But there is nothing to guarantee that this will happen, and it may not happen for several years in your state.

This situation is made worse by the fact that if you must pay a hefty state capital gains tax, it could push you into an alternative minimum tax (AMT) situation in which you would now owe additional federal taxes! Check with your accountant on this.

As of this writing, many states are beginning the process of changing their tax laws to mirror those of the federal government. By September, for example, California's legislature had changed the rules retroactively back to May 7, 1997. The situation may be similar in your state.

:: HINT ::

Check with your accountant when planning the sale of a principal residence. You may want to wait until your state enacts laws mirroring those of the federal government so that you can avoid paying state capital gains taxes and, at least potentially, avoid federal AMT.

—❚—

CHAPTER FIVE

What if I Claim a Portion of My Home as a Home Office?

THE HOME OFFICE deduction has been on the books for many years; however, until the 1997 tax reduction bill, its use was extremely strict. The new tax law makes it more liberal for some taxpayers.

In this chapter we'll look at the home office deduction and how to combine it with the up to $500,000 exclusion for maximum tax advantage.

What Is a Home Office Deduction?

Basically this rule states that you may claim a portion of the cost of maintaining an office in your principal residence (even if it is a rental) as a business expense, provided you meet strict qualifying rules. When you are able to claim this expense, you can then deduct a portion of it from your business income. For example, if you are renting your principal residence, you may deduct a portion of your rent. If you own your principal residence, you may be able to deduct a portion of your mortgage interest, taxes, utilities, and other costs of ownership. In addition, you may depreciate that portion of the home that is devoted to the office. As a result, a home office can result in a substantial business income tax deduction.

What Are the Basic Rules for Deducting a Home Office?

The basic rules are quite strict. First, with regard to the space itself, it must be used exclusively for the purpose of a business office. No dual-purpose use is allowed.

For example, if you have a four-bedroom home, you may use one room (or two rooms, or as many rooms as appropriate) exclusively as your home office. However, you cannot occasionally use the same room(s) for sleeping, for watching recreational television, or for any other activity. The space must be strictly a home office.

Similarly, if you occasionally use the dining room table to work on business matters, you cannot claim that area as a home office since its use is not exclusive.

Second, the amount of the deduction you can take is determined by the percentage of space the home office occupies. For example, if you're using one bedroom of 150 square feet in a four-bedroom house with 2000 square feet, you are using 7.5 percent of the house as a home office. You would, therefore, be able to deduct as a business expense 7.5 percent of the housing costs including taxes, mortgage interest, utilities, and so on. If your principal residence were a rental, you could deduct 7.5 percent of your rent plus a similar percentage of utilities.

Third, according to the old rules, a majority of your business services must be performed within your home office. This was a real stickler for many self-employed taxpayers who run their businesses from their homes but perform services on the road.

For example, you might have a carpet cleaning service. You advertise and receive phone calls in your home office.

You order supplies from there and do all your billing and paperwork there. But your actual business service—cleaning carpets—is done in other people's homes or businesses.

Or you're a salesperson. You have a home office where you discuss business with clients. You take orders over your home office phone and order deliveries of products over the same phone. You do all your accounting and paperwork at the home office. But, as a salesperson, you spend 70 percent of your time on the road finding new customers and dealing directly with old customers.

Since the majority of your time as a carpet cleaner or salesperson or other similarly self-employed individual is spent away from the home, under the old rules you could not claim a home office business deduction.

What Are the New Rules?

Under the new rules you are no longer required to perform most of your business services in the home office. You can still clean carpets, sell products, or whatever outside of the home office and claim it as a business deduction.

However, it's important to understand that this liberalization does not take effect until 1999. For the taxable years of 1997 and 1998, you must still perform most of your services in the home office for it to be deductible.

What Problems Do I Face with a Home Office When I Sell My Home?

A home office is a business. A principal residence is not. Therefore, when you sell a principal residence in which you have a home office, two different sets of rules apply.

As noted above, you must first determine what portion of the property is the principal residence and what portion is the home office. Using the example above, 92.5 percent is the principal residence. Therefore, assuming it (and you) otherwise qualify, 92.5 percent of the capital gain on the sale is excluded up to the new $500,000 maximum.

The remaining 7.5 percent of the capital gain, however, is taxed at the capital gains rate, usually 20 percent.

What this means, therefore, is that if you maintain a home office, when you sell your property you will not be able to exclude all of your capital gain, even if it is within the $500,000 maximum. A certain portion will be considered taxable because of the home office.

Is There Any Way to Avoid This Problem?

Yes, there is. But you have to think ahead.

If you are anticipating selling your principal residence in which you maintain a home office, do not claim the home office for the tax year before you sell.

It's true you will not get the business expense deduction you might otherwise qualify for. However, when it comes time to sell, you will not have to pay tax on that portion of your capital gain that would be attributed to a home office, because you won't have one.

:: HINT ::

The exclusion apparently does not apply to depreciation taken during the time you owned a home and used it as a business or as a rental. Check with your accountant.

This is one of those situations where it probably will help to break out a calculator and figure out which way you save the most. If you have trouble with the figures, your accountant should be able to calculate them for you quickly and easily.

Capital Gain Reduction

CHAPTER SIX

Effect of Capital Gains Tax on Investment

HE 1997 TAX REDUCTION ACT lowered the tax on capital gains. However, capital gains are now taxed in a more complex way than ever before in this country.

While previously we had a capital gains tax rate of up to 28 percent, we now have a variety of rates—20 percent on appreciated property, 25 percent on depreciated real estate, 10 percent for low-income taxpayers, and a further reduction to come in the future to levels of 18 percent and 8 percent.

Needless to say, the new capital gains tax rate is bewildering to many people. However, I hope to clarify it in the next few chapters. First, though, let's take a look at how the capital gains tax can influence investment decisions.

What Was the Old Capital Gains Tax Rate?

Over the years the federal government has repeatedly tinkered with the capital gains tax rate. Depending on the prevailing economic and political philosophy, the rate has gone up and down. Here's a chart showing the changes since

1960. Note that in the recent past the rate has been much higher than at the present time, but not lower.

Effective Capital Gains Tax Rate

1960	25%
1968	27%
1969	28%
1971	34%
1972	45%
1976	49%
1979	28%
1981	20%
1987	28%
1988	33%
1991	28%
1997	20% (or less)

Source: U.S. Chamber of Commerce.

What Influence Does the Capital Gains Rate Have on Real Estate Investment?

If the tax rate on real estate is significantly lower than the tax rate on ordinary income, it encourages people to invest in real estate. To put it another way, if we take the new capital gains tax rate as only 20 percent and the maximum marginal tax rate on ordinary income for an individual as 39.6 percent, it should be obvious that wherever possible, investors will have a strong desire to characterize income as capital gain to save on taxes. In short, a much lower capital gains tax rate should have a significant influence in the marketplace.

Note from this chart that previously the differential between the top marginal tax rate on ordinary income and

OLD   NEW

← Maximum tax 39.6%

11.6% difference

Capital gains rate 28%

19.6% difference

Capital gains rate 20%

the capital gains rate paid on the sale of real estate was roughly 11 percent. Now, however, that differential has jumped to roughly 19 percent. In fact, the capital gains tax rate is now about half the maximum tax rate on ordinary income.

If we translate this into personal terms, it comes out something like the following. In recent years many people have felt: "Why should I sell my investment property if I'm going to have to give the government nearly a third of my gain in taxes? I'd rather hang on to it or seek another alternative" (such as trading—see Chapter 10).

On the other hand, with the new capital gains rate now down to 20 percent for many people, put in personal terms, investors may feel like this: "If I sell my investment property, I will pay only a fifth of its appreciated value in taxes. Maybe selling makes sense now."

> **:: HINT ::**
>
> It's interesting to recall that during the Reagan years, when the capital gains rate and the regular rate were virtually the same, the concept of a capital gain became irrelevant. However, all areas of the tax code dealing with calculations, concepts, and so on of capital gains were kept intact. Someone apparently knew the differential would be back!

Of course, most people don't have the flexibility to choose between receiving regular income or investing in real estate to take advantage of the reduced capital gains tax rate. But some people do, and their incentives have just skyrocketed.

> **:: HINT ::**
>
> Now that capital gain is taxed even more favorably than before when compared to ordinary income, the Internal Revenue Service can be expected to be more vigilant in applying its code provisions with regard to the characterization of income as a capital gain.

The Recapture of Depreciation

Unfortunately, there's one fly in the ointment and that's the fact that the new law has a special 25 percent tax rate on capital gain attributed to the recapture of depreciation. This refers to the depreciation taken over the course of ownership of an investment property and is discussed in greater detail in Chapters 7 and 9. For now, however, let's just consider the effect of this higher capital gains tax rate.

In the past, investors tended to buy and hold real estate. The idea was to find a good property, rent it out for years while appreciation slowly occurred, and then sell for a profit.

Now, however, there's a possible penalty associated with holding onto that property for a period of time. The longer you hold it, the more it depreciates, and the more it depreciates, the higher the capital gains tax rate you'll pay on sale (25 percent versus 10 or 20 percent).

Therefore, from an economic perspective, for some investors it may make more sense to buy, hold for the minimum period (18 months), and then resell as soon as possible. These investors will thus be looking more for property with rapid price appreciation potential than that with long-term staying power. What we may indeed see is the development of a kind of "musical chairs" situation in real estate where investors bail out of properties in less than two years, buy new ones, and then repeat the process.

Unfortunately, this is reminiscent of investors in stocks who look for companies that can show a profit within the next few quarters as opposed to those companies whose profits may be flat, but that are building long term for the future. Or, to put it another way, the waste society, where items are quickly consumed and discarded, may have just come to real estate.

✄ HINT ✄

When the capital gains tax rate is too high, it causes people to change their economic decisions, and that warps the real estate market. A low capital gains rate tends to make real estate transactions more economically sound.

Do Changes in the Tax Laws Contribute to the Recent Real Estate Ups and Downs?

The biggest real estate recession in this country since the Great Depression began approximately three to four years after the Tax Reform Act of 1986 came into being. That act, among other things, produced some very unfavorable rulings with regard to real estate, perhaps the most stringent being that it reduced the tax shelter potential of real estate investments by recharacterizing real estate as a "passive activity," losses resulting from which could no longer be easily deducted from the ordinary income of high-income taxpayers.

While it would be difficult to conclude that the real estate recession was caused primarily by the 1986 Tax Reform Act (which would fail to take into account an overall economic recession at the same time), it would probably be incorrect to likewise assume that it had no influence at all. Indeed, tax law changes do have a big influence on how and whether investors invest in real estate.

Will the 1997 Tax Relief Act Cause a Real Estate Boom or Bust?

Similarly, it can be expected that the 1997 Tax Relief Act will also have a significant (though perhaps difficult-to-measure) effect on real estate. Many real estate watchers, in fact, have predicted that an early increase in the number of properties for sale will cause at least a temporary slump in the market. (As of this writing, I have not yet seen evidence of this happening.)

Others, on the other hand, predict a robust market as investors move more quickly between properties to take advantage of the new 20 percent rate. Similarly, the up to $500,000 exclusion could cause high-end taxpayers to sell their residences whenever appreciation approaches the $500,000 limit.

Certainly, the new capital gains tax will bend involvement in real estate both up and down as investors seek to take the best advantage of the new law.

CHAPTER SEVEN

The Changes in the Capital Gains Law

T HERE'S GOOD NEWS and there's bad news.

The good news is that the capital gains tax has been reduced. This should prove beneficial to everyone who invests in real estate.

The bad news is that the new rules are very complicated. For example, now there are five capital gains tax rates.

10 percent	For those in the 15 percent tax bracket
20 percent	For those in higher tax brackets
25 percent (maximum)	For the recapture of depreciation
28 percent (maximum)	For midterm gains
39.6 percent (maximum)	For short-term holding periods

In addition, beginning after the year 2000 there will be two additional rates for property held five years or more.

8 percent	For those in the 15 percent tax bracket

18 percent	For those in higher tax brackets and for properties acquired after 2001

Sound confusing? It is!

While the following chapters in this section will cover the basics and endeavor to explain the new capital gains tax rules, this material should be considered strictly an overview. Unless you are very savvy in tax matters, it is suggested that for the actual preparation of your own taxes you consult a tax specialist. This is true even if you elect to do your taxes using one of the various computer programs available.

Getting Started

To understand how the new capital gains tax works, it is first necessary to cover some information that may be old hat for many readers, but confusing to others. I'm speaking of marginal tax rates: what they are and how they work. If you understand this concept, please feel free to move on to the next section. However, if marginal tax rates confuse you, read on.

What Is My Tax Bracket?

How much tax you'll pay and your actual tax savings under the old versus the new rules will depend on how big your capital gain is and your tax bracket. There are new capital gains tax rates based on your marginal income tax bracket.

What is a marginal tax bracket? As those familiar with federal income taxes know, there are currently five tax brackets, ranging from a low of 0 percent to a high of 39.6 percent. These are *marginal brackets*, which means in essence that as you earn more money, you move into a higher bracket and a greater percentage of your income is taxed. But the higher bracket only covers money you earn beyond the margin of the lower bracket.

EXAMPLE

If you're married and filing jointly, your taxable income (after all exemptions, allowances, deductions, and so on) between $0 and $41,200 is taxed at a 15 percent rate.

If you make more than that amount, you still pay 15 percent on the income up to $41,200, but you also pay 28 percent on the income between $41,200 and $99,600.

And the rate goes up as you make more money and enter higher tax brackets.

Here are the tax rates for a married couple filing jointly and for singles.

⬚ TAX BRACKETS ⬚

The following chart shows ordinary income tax rates (*not* capital gains rates) you may have to pay on your income from salary, dividends, and so on. Note that the rates shown are for 1997. Rates are indexed for inflation and tend to rise each year.

Federal Annual Tax Rates for Married Couples

$0 to $ 41,200	15%
$ 41,201 to $ 99,600	28%
$ 99,601 to $151,750	31%
$151,751 to $271,050	36%
$271,051 and higher	39.6%

Federal Annual Tax Rates for Singles

$0 to $ 24,650	15%
$ 24,651 to $ 59,750	28%
$ 59,751 to $124,650	31%
$124,651 to $271,050	36%
$271,051 and higher	39.6%

Note that the essence of the marginal tax bracket system is that the rate of tax you pay increases along with your income. But everyone still pays the lowest tax on their first dollars of income. Even though you may be, for example, in the 31 percent tax bracket, as a married person filing jointly you still pay only 15 percent on your income up to $41,200, 28 percent on income between $41,200 and $99,600, and 31 percent only on the balance above $99,600. Only your "last dollars" are taxed at the highest rate. Your "first dollars" are still taxed at the lower rates.

❊ ❊ ❊
EXAMPLE

I am in the 28 percent tax bracket. Does that mean that I pay 28 percent in taxes to the federal government?

Answer: No. You pay 28 percent only on your taxable income above $41,200 as a married person filing jointly. If your total income is $78,000, then you pay much less than 28 percent. In your case, the actual rate of tax you pay is a blending of the two brackets. You are paying 15 percent on the first $41,200 and 28 percent on the last $36,800. Your true tax rate is thus 21.5 percent.

Calculating Your True Tax Rate

$41,200	→ 15%	=	$6,180	1st bracket
$41,200–$78,000	→ 28%	=	$10,304	2nd bracket
$78,000	→ 21%	=	$16,484	true tax rate

❊ ❊ ❊

You're never taxed more than 15 percent, in the case of a married couple filing jointly or qualifying widow(er), on the first $41,200 you make, no matter how high your total income. But on money over that margin, you're taxed at the higher rate of 28 percent until you reach the next bracket. In part, that's why it's called a progressive income tax. The more you make, the greater the rate at which you pay. The tax progresses upward. (It's also called progressive because it supposedly is socially forward-looking in its approach.)

How Was the Capital Gains Tax Calculated the Old Way?

Now let's move on to the capital gains tax.

In the past, when you sold real estate, whether it was a single-family rental or a large commercial center, and had a capital gain (as explained in the previous chapter), the rate for an individual (as opposed to a corporation) on a capital gain was the lowest of that person's marginal tax rates or a maximum of 28 percent. The best way to understand this is to walk through a calculation.

Assuming that you were taxed as an individual (not a corporation), you'd take the capital gain that you made and simply add it to your ordinary income. Then you'd calculate the marginal tax bracket this put you in and compare it to the old maximum capital gains tax rate of 28 percent.

If your ordinary income bracket was the lowest (15 percent), then the portion of your capital gain that remained in that bracket would be taxed at the lower of either 15 percent or 28 percent—obviously, at 15 percent.

EXAMPLE

Your regular income was $20,000. You had a $15,000 capital gain. What was your capital gains tax?

Answer: **You added your $15,000 capital gain to your $20,000 income and discovered that you were still in the 15 percent tax bracket. Therefore the tax on your capital gain was 15 percent.**

On the other hand, if your bracket was pushed higher by the addition of the capital gain, the amount you'd pay on that gain could still never be more than 28 percent.

⠿ ⠿ ⠿

EXAMPLE

Your regular income was $80,000. You had a $200,000 capital gain. Adding the two together gave you a total of $280,000. How much was your capital tax rate?

Answer: Using the 1997 rates for a married person filing jointly, you would owe 28 percent on the first $19,600 (up to the 31 percent bracket) of the capital gain; the lesser of 28 percent or 31 percent on the balance up to $151,750 (up to the 36 percent bracket); the lesser of 28 percent or 36 percent on the balance up to $271,050 (up to the 39.6 percent bracket); and the lesser of 28 percent or 39.6 percent on the remainder.

Your maximum capital gains tax rate was 28 percent. Under the old rules you could never pay more than 28 percent on a capital gain.

Tax on $80,000 of Ordinary Income

$41,200 @ 15% = $ 6,180
$38,800 @ 28% = $10,864

$80,000 $17,044

Tax on $200,000 Capital Gain

$200,000 @ 28% = $56,000

total tax $73,044

(Note: If it weren't for the capital gains tax limit of 28 percent, you would have paid $85,191 in total taxes.)

⠿ ⠿ ⠿

Remember, if you sold a property and had a capital gain, that capital gain was first lumped in with your ordinary income (from salary or dividends). If, even with that added income from the sale of a property, your marginal tax rate stayed at 15 percent, that was tax you paid. If, on the other hand, it did rise higher, say to 36 percent, then the maximum capital gains rate applied and you paid only 28 percent. Let's take a few more examples to be sure we're clear on how the old system worked:

EXAMPLE

You were a married taxpayer filing jointly having no taxable ordinary income (from salary or dividends). But you did have a home and sold it for a capital gain of $30,000. What was the tax on this gain?

Answer: The lowest marginal tax rate applies up to incomes of $41,200 and is set at 15 percent. Therefore your tax on all your capital gain would have been 15 percent.

EXAMPLE

You were a married taxpayer filing jointly having no taxable income from salary. But you sold a home, realizing a capital gain of $200,000. What was the rate at which you would have paid taxes?

Answer: You would pay a 15 percent rate on the amount up to $41,200. Then 28 percent up to $99,600, the next marginal tax rate. The marginal tax rates after that are 31 percent up to $151,750 and 36 percent above that to $271,050. However, because your income of $200,000 was all a capital gain, the balance above $41,200 would be taxed at a maximum of 28 percent, the former capital gains tax rate. You never paid more than 28 percent

***

From the above examples, it should be clear how the old capital gains tax worked. Now let's look at the new rules. It's a bit more complicated today.

The New 20 Percent Tax Rate

The new maximum capital gains tax is divided between gain that comes from appreciation to the property and gain that comes from the recapture of depreciation previously taken. We will discuss the recapture of depreciation at the end of this chapter and also in the next chapter. Here we are *only* going to be concerned with capital gain attributed to appreciation with no depreciation involved.

The top rate is 20 percent. This is the maximum rate at which you will pay tax on an appreciated capital gain. It replaces the earlier 28 percent rate noted previously. This represents a 29 percent reduction in the maximum capital gains tax rate. Note that this is the *top* rate. There is a bottom capital gains rate, which we will get into in a moment.

***

EXAMPLE

Your ordinary income is $50,000 a year. You get an appreciated capital gain of $200,000. What is your capital gains tax rate?

Answer: You are already in the 28 percent tax bracket. The new top 20 percent rate applies. You pay 20 percent ($40,000) of your capital gains in taxes.

***

What if I'm in a Lower Tax Bracket?

What should be evident is that the lowest tax bracket (15 percent) is less than the maximum capital gains tax rate (20 percent). To benefit those in this lowest marginal tax bracket, the capital gains tax actually has a second, bottom rate of 10 percent. Therefore, the lowest capital gains tax rate is actually 10 percent. This benefit is of limited value, however, for as soon as the capital gain added to the taxpayer's income hits the next tax bracket, the 20 percent rate applies.

EXAMPLE

I'm married and file jointly. I make $20,000 a year and therefore am in the lowest (15 percent) tax bracket. I have a rental house, which I sell, realizing a $15,000 capital gain. How much tax do I pay?

Answer: **The calculation here is fairly simple. You would add the capital gains to your regular income for a total of $35,000. Since this full amount is still within the 15 percent marginal tax bracket, you would pay ordinary income tax on your regular income ($20,000 at 15 percent) and you would pay the bottom capital gains tax rate on your full capital gain (10 percent on the $15,000 capital gain).**

The calculation gets more complex when there's a larger capital gain.

EXAMPLE

I'm also married filing jointly. I make $30,000 a year and also am in the lowest (15 percent) tax bracket. I sell a rental duplex and realize a $60,000 gain. What is the capital gains tax rate I would pay?

Answer: The calculation is fairly complex. You would add the capital gain to your regular income. As much of the capital gain as remains in the 15 percent tax bracket would be taxed at the bottom 10 percent rate. As soon as the capital gain boosts you into the next marginal tax bracket, at $41,200 (the 28 percent marginal tax bracket), you would begin paying capital gains tax at the top rate (20 percent).

Ordinary income	$30,000	15% rate
Capital gain to a maximum of $41,200	$11,200	10% rate
Capital gain over $41,200 bracket	$48,800	20% rate

In other words, you would pay 10 percent on the first $11,200 of the capital gain and 20 percent on the balance.

\#\# \#\#

What if I'm in a *Middle* Tax Bracket?

If you're in a middle income tax bracket before capital gains, from 28 to 31 percent, the calculation for your appreciated capital gains tax is straightforward. Since you have ordinary income moving you up into higher brackets, the new 20 percent top rate applies.

\#\# \#\#

EXAMPLE

I make $100,000 a year. I sell a commercial building and realize a $150,000 capital gain. What rate do I pay on my capital gain? Does it affect the rate I pay on my ordinary income?

Answer: You'd pay a 20 percent rate on your capital gain. Since your ordinary income is already in the 31 percent bracket, it is unaffected by the capital gain.

※ ※ ※

What if I'm in the Top Tax Bracket?

If you are in the 39.6 percent tax bracket, you will save a great deal of money by paying capital gains tax. It will be roughly half the rate of the last dollars in your marginal bracket.

※ ※ ※

EXAMPLE

In the top bracket you will pay 39.6 percent on your last dollars of income. However, you'll only pay 20 percent on a capital gain. The difference is roughly half.

※ ※ ※

Isn't There a New Holding Period?

Indeed there is. In the past, the holding period for a long-term capital gain was 12 months. The new holding period for a long-term capital gain is 18 months. There is also a new midterm capital gain holding period, discussed in the following section.

The new longer long-term holding period is likely to have a stronger impact on investors in other capital assets, notably stocks, than it is on those involved in real estate. The reason is that the holding period for real estate investments (for economic reasons) is typically longer than the corresponding periods for most other investments.

What Is the New Midterm Holding Period?

There is now also a new midterm capital gain holding period. It's for assets held for less than 18 months but more than 12 months. The old up to 28 percent capital gains rate is the one used here.

What about Short Term?

The rate for a short-term capital gain of 12 months or less remains the same as before—the capital gain is added to the investor's regular income and taxed at the ordinary income rate. You get no capital gains tax benefit on assets held less than 12 months.

:: HINT ::

Don't get confused between investment property, which we are discussing here, and sale of a principal residence, covered in the last section. While there is no short-term capital gain tax rate benefit on investment property, the same is not necessarily true if it's your main home. You'll recall that for a principal residence where you are forced to sell in less than two years because of influences beyond your control (page 21), you may still use a portion of the up to $250,000 per person exclusion.

:: :: ::

EXAMPLE

I buy a rental house and after nine months get a terrific offer. I sell, realizing a $100,000 capital gain. What is the tax rate I must pay?

Answer: Because you held the property for less than 12 months, it is considered a short-term capital gain. Therefore, your entire capital gain is added to your other ordinary income and taxed at normal income tax rates (up to 39.6 percent).

EXAMPLE

I buy a rental house and sell after 14 months. I realize a $100,000 capital gain. What tax rate must I pay?

Answer: The maximum midterm capital gain rate for properties held for between 12 and 18 months is 28 percent. In essence, you would pay capital gains tax at the old rates.

EXAMPLE

I buy a rental home and hold it for two years. I sell and that portion of my capital gain attributable to appreciation is $100,000. What rate do I pay?

Answer: You would pay a maximum rate of 20 percent because you had held the property for the minimum 18-month period.

Will This Holding Period Change in a Few Years?

No, the minimum holding period remains in force until and unless there's a new change in the tax code.

However, there is a separate holding period that applies after December 31, 2000. For real estate acquired after that date and *held for five years*, the top capital gains rate will be reduced to 18 percent. The reduction for those in the 15 percent tax bracket will be to a bottom rate of 8 percent, but it appears that the property at this lower rate does not have to be acquired after 2001. Check with your accountant.

EXAMPLE

I purchase a rental property in 2001 and hold it for five years, until 2006, when I sell it for a $300,000 capital gain, all due to appreciation. What is my tax rate?

Answer: Since the property was held for at least five years after the qualifying date, you add the gain to your ordinary income and that portion of it that is in the 15 percent marginal tax bracket is taxed at an 8 percent rate. That portion of it that puts you into a higher tax bracket is taxed at an 18 percent rate.

EXAMPLE

I make $20,000 a year and in the year 2007 will have a capital gain due to appreciation of $15,000. What is my tax rate?

Answer: Assuming that the same tax brackets were in effect and that the property was held for five years, your rate of capital gains tax would be 8 percent or $1,200.

:: :: ::

EXAMPLE

What if, in the same example as above, my ordinary income is $30,000?

Answer: Again assuming that the same tax brackets were in effect and that the property was purchased after December 31, 2000 and held for at least five years, your rate would be 8 percent of the amount of the gain between $30,000 and $41,200 and 18 percent of the balance.

Property Held over Five Years after 12/31/2000

(Note: the following is based on 1997 tax rates. Presumably they will have been indexed higher by the year 2001.)

Ordinary income	$30,000	15% rate
Capital gain to a maximum of $41,200	$11,200	8% rate
Capital gain over $41,200 bracket	$48,800	18% rate (acquired after 12/31/2000)

:: :: ::

:: HINT ::

Remember, when calculating the tax rate for a capital gain, your regular income is not taxed any differently than it would otherwise be. When you add the capital gain to it, it is just for the purpose of determining the rate at which the capital gain is taxed.

What about the Recapture of Depreciation?

At the beginning of this chapter I noted that what we were describing applied only to capital gain due to appreciation. However, virtually all investment real estate is depreciated. The rate of depreciation varies, usually depending on the maximum depreciation allowed by law at the time the property was purchased (put into service).

** HINT **

Only improvements to the property, the building, roads, fences, and so on, are depreciated. Land is not depreciated.

Under the new law there is a separate category for a capital gain due to depreciation. The tax rate is 25 percent. This is separate from the other capital gains rates we have been discussing (the 20 percent and 10 percent rates), which apply to appreciation.

The depreciation subject to capital gain previously taken during the entire life of the property (your ownership of it) is added up at the time of the sale and is taxed at the new 25 percent rate.

** ** **

EXAMPLE

You are in the top tax bracket, purchase an apartment building, and hold it for seven years, depreciating it at the rate of $10,000 a year (straight line method). Now you sell. At the time of the sale your total depreciation on the apartment building is $70,000. What tax will you pay on that depreciation when you sell?

Answer: All of the recaptured depreciation is taxed at a rate of 25 percent, for a total tax of $17,500.

※ ※ ※

※ ※ ※

EXAMPLE

You are in the top tax bracket and purchase an apartment building and hold it for seven years, depreciating it at the rate of $10,000 a year (straight line method). Now you sell for a total capital gain of $150,000. At the time of the sale your total depreciation on the apartment building is $70,000. What capital gains tax will you pay on the sale?

Answer: You will pay 25 percent on the recapture of the $70,000 due to depreciation and 20 percent on the remaining $80,000 due to appreciation.

※ ※ ※

The recapture of depreciation is the most difficult aspect of the new law to grasp. We will go into it in detail in Chapter 9.

What Are the Effective Dates of the New Law?

The new law was written so that the effective date was May 6, 1997, when the original budget compromise bill was agreed on. However, because it took an additional two months to iron out all the details, the actual law did not pass Congress until July 28, 1997. Therefore, there is some confusion about which dates apply and what the capital gains rates will be during those dates.

Properties Sold Prior to May 6, 1997

If you sold your investment property prior to May 6, 1997, the old rules apply. You will pay up to a maximum of 28 percent tax on any capital gain calculated the old-fashioned way.

Properties Sold between May 6 and July 28, 1997

If you sold between these two dates, a separate set of rules applies. This was a compromise to satisfy those who relied on the comments of the chairmen of the congressional tax-writing committees involved in creating the law. Generally speaking, you will use the old 12-month qualifying period for a long-term capital gain, but will be able to use the new 20 percent maximum tax rate.

Properties Sold July 29, 1997 and Later

The new holding periods (18 months for long term and 12 to 18 months for midterm) and rates apply.

What Was Not Included in the New Tax Law?

There has been some confusion about what was not included in the new tax law. A number of provisions were discussed early on that did not meet the approval of Congress or the president. These were eliminated, but may be resurrected at some time in the future in new tax bills. They are included here so that those who were aware of them may take note.

Indexing Due to Inflation

Everyone knows that in good times the price of real estate goes up and up. But is that appreciation in price due to an actual increase in intrinsic value, or is it simply an increase due to the loss of value in our currency? Real estate is a commodity, like pork chops or gold, and as a commodity is subject to the influence of inflation. If inflation goes up by 3 percent a year and that is reflected by a 3 percent increase in property values, should that increase be taxed as a capital gain when the property is sold?

Many investors and members of Congress think not. Rather, they argue, the inflation factor should be cut out of the capital gains calculation. The property should be indexed so that each year, for the purposes of calculating a capital gain, a certain portion of appreciation is eliminated.

As explained, this indexing due to inflation did not pass, but is still a viable contender in some circles. It is explained in greater detail in Appendix B.

A Lower Capital Gains Tax Rate

While the reduction from 28 percent to 20 percent was widely hailed, the celebration tends to obscure the fact that the original proposals included a far lower rate. Indeed, in the 1995 tax proposal, which passed Congress but was not signed by the President, the capital gains tax rate would have been reduced to 14 percent—half of the old rate. It is not inconceivable that the capital gains tax rate could be lowered at some point in the future.

CHAPTER EIGHT

——✠——

How to Calculate
Your Capital Gain

YOU ONLY REALIZE a capital gain when you sell your
property. Of course, given the real estate market over
the last few years, you might realize a capital loss, but that's a
subject to be covered separately. Assuming that you sell for
more than you paid, chances are you probably have a capital
gain. This is true whether the property was your principal
residence or a rental (business or trade) property.

We've already seen in the preceding chapters how the new
up to $500,000 exclusion benefits those with a capital gain
on a principal residence. In later chapters we'll see how the
reduced tax on a capital gain is calculated on investment
property. Here, however, we're going to go over some of the
basics of determining just how big a capital gain you may
have.

:: HINT ::

Capital gain is calculated in the same way whether the property is a rental (trade or business property) or a principal residence. What's different is that there is an up to $500,000 exclusion, for marrieds filing jointly, on a principal residence that does not exist for rentals (trade or business property).

For those who have at least a smidgen of an accounting background, this will be quite simple. For those who don't have that background, watch closely. It's not done with mirrors, but it does take a bit of concentration to catch.

What's the Difference between Capital Gain and Profit?

It's convenient for many people to think of *profit* and *capital gain* as synonymous terms. They often are not. *Profit* is a rather loose term that most of us use to indicate how much money we think we made when we sell a property: "I bought a rental house for $100,000 and sold it for $150,000 — I had a profit of $50,000." *Capital gain,* on the other hand, is a technical term calculated in a very specific way by the Internal Revenue Service (IRS). While the profit may indeed be $50,000, the capital gain may be quite a different figure — higher or lower.

Capital gain is actually the difference between the tax basis in your property and what you sell the property for after deducting your costs of sale. *Basis* is the operative word here, and you must understand it in order to understand the calculation for capital gains.

What Is Basis?

Basis is essentially what you are into a property for. It usually begins with the purchase price (sometimes construction costs), and from that other items are added and subtracted.

⛄ ⛄ ⛄
EXAMPLE

You buy a single-family home to rent out. You put down 20 percent or $20,000 in cash. You get a new mortgage for $70,000 and assume an existing second mortgage for $10,000. Your equity in the property is the $20,000 you put in. But your cost for calculating basis includes cash put down, new loans, and assumption of existing mortgages. Therefore you begin calculating your basis at $100,000. The amount of the mortgages is included in the basis.

⛄ ⛄ ⛄

What about My Purchase Expenses?

You almost certainly had some expenses involved as part of the purchase. Many of these expenses, particularly those that are nonrecurring, can be added to your basis. (Recurring costs are such things as taxes, insurance, and so on, that come up over and over again.)

Here are some of the nonrecurring costs that you may have had as part of the purchase of the property.

- Title insurance fees
- Escrow charges
- Agent fees (for a buyer's agent, if you used one, or seller's agent, if you agreed to pay some or all of the seller's costs)

- A survey to determine the exact setting of the property
- Transfer taxes, if any
- Assumption costs for a seller's mortgage including back taxes, recording fees, and so on
- Improvements to the property, made prior to the sale by the seller, for which you agree to pay
- Legal charges, including fees for preparing the deed and the purchase aggreement
- Special assessments for improvements
- Other nondeductible expense (for example, you would not add the cost of earthquake insurance)

As you can see, your basis in the property is considerably more than simply the purchase price. In some cases the basis may be 5 percent or more higher than the purchase price, all coming just from the expenses of the purchase.

▌▌▌
EXAMPLE

You purchase a home for $125,000 and pay $3,000 in closing costs including title insurance, escrow fees, document fees, and transfer taxes. There is also $700 in property tax prorations and fire insurance. Plus you pay $1500 to a broker as a buyer's agent's fee. What is your tax basis?

Purchase price	$125,000
Nondeductible expenses (title insurance, escrow, etc.)	$ 3,000
Broker's fee	$ 1,500
Tax basis	$129,500

Note that you could not add the $700 in property tax prorations and fire insurance fees to your basis.

(However, if it's an investment property, you may take these as a deduction to offset rental income in determining your annual profit or loss. If it's your home, you may take the property taxes as a deduction, but not the insurance premium.)

:: :: ::

:: TAX PLANNING ::

It's to your advantage to get the basis in your property as high as possible. Remember, the capital gain is the spread between the basis and the sales price less selling costs. The higher the basis, the smaller the capital gain (on which you'll owe taxes).

What's My Basis When I Build a Home?

Sometimes your basis in a property will be determined by other factors. For example, say you buy a lot and then build a house on it. What is your tax basis?

Your basis will be your price for the lot (including costs of purchase) plus interest on your construction loan (if you have one) during the construction period, plus the cost of construction.

:: :: ::

EXAMPLE

If you buy a lot for $50,000 plus $2,500 in purchase costs and then build a home on it for $100,000 plus $5,000 in interest, your basis at the time your property is finished would be $157,500.

Lot price .... $ 50,000
Purchase costs .... $ 2,500

Construction costs $100,000

Construction interest .... $ 5,000

Tax basis $157,500

⌗ ⌗ ⌗

Does My Basis Ever Change?

Your tax basis can change during your ownership in several ways. Two of the most common ways are the cost of fixing up the property after a casualty loss (such as hurricane or earthquake damage) or additions to the property that you make after the purchase. Let's consider the second more carefully.

You can increase your tax basis by improving your property. Of course, the improvements have to be a capital investment. That means that, for example, if it's a rental, trade, or business property, they cannot be deducted from rental income as an expense. Here's a list of some of the improvements that can be used to increase your basis.

Ways You Increase Your Tax Basis

- Installing a new driveway
- Adding another bathroom
- Putting on a new roof
- Adding permanent shrubs and trees (as opposed to seasonal flowers)
- Building a patio, deck, or wall
- Landscaping
- Putting in a swimming pool or spa
- Installing new plumbing or electrical wiring
- Adding a new furnace or air conditioning system

- Storm windows (permanent ones)
- Legal fees involved in defending your title or improving the property (such as having the zoning changed)

In addition, if you buy a fixer-upper and renovate it, most of the costs involved are added to your basis.

:: TAX HINT ::

Remember, if it's maintenance, it's generally not a capital improvement and hence is not added to your basis. (While maintenance may be deducted from income if the property is a rental, trade, or business property, maintenance or repair to a principal residence is not deductible and does not add to basis.)

You can also lower your tax basis.

Ways You Lower Your Tax Basis

- Taking depreciation
- Theft and casualty losses
- Granting easements
- Under the old tax rules, adding gain from the sale from your old home when rolling it over

Does Depreciation Lower My Basis?

Thus far we've been talking about different factors that cause the tax basis to go up. However, there are other factors that cause the tax basis to go down, including a casualty loss to the property (a portion of it burns down) or depreciation.

Depreciation is the reduction in value of a capital asset, in this case a rental property, over time. (Note: only the improved portion of the property—the house, not the lot—is depreciated.) Depreciation is a very important consideration because the new Taxpayer Relief Act treats capital gain due to depreciation differently from capital gain due to price appreciation (20 percent versus 25 percent tax).

You cannot depreciate your principal residence; hence this is not usually an issue where principal residences are concerned. (The exception is when you have converted a principal residence to a rental or vice versa, which will be covered later.) Thus, what we are concerned about here is the depreciation on investment real estate.

When you depreciate your rental real estate, you reduce your basis by the amount of the depreciation taken each year.

:: TAX HINT ::

Depreciation lowers the tax basis.

:: :: ::
EXAMPLE

Let's say you have a rental property with a tax basis of $200,000, on which your mortgage interest (not including principal reduction), taxes, and all operating expenses come to $10,000 for the year. Your income from rents also comes to $10,000, making it a wash in terms of cash flow. You have no cash profit or loss.

However, you now make an accounting calculation; you depreciate the property by $4000 on paper. (It's called a *paper loss* because no cash passed out of your hands. Indeed, the property may well have gone up in actual value during the year.)

You now must lower your tax basis by the amount of the depreciation. In this case your tax basis goes down from $200,000 to a new adjusted basis of $196,000.

Original tax basis	$200,000
Less depreciation	–$ 4,000
Adjusted tax basis	$196,000

:: :: ::

> ## :: HINT ::
> It is not mandatory that you claim depreciation each year. But even if you don't claim it each year, it is still deducted from basis when the calculation for gain or loss is made. The rule in the tax code reads "allowed or allowable" since acquisition. Of course, this does not apply to a personal residence.

Doesn't Depreciation Help Me Out on My Annual Income Taxes?

Yes, it can. Depreciation is considered an investment expense on a rental property, just like advertising, mortgages, and taxes. In that it adds to a loss during the year, it can help to reduce your income taxes.

:: TAX HINT ::

According to the tax code, rental property is considered passive income for tax purposes, and a passive income loss normally *cannot* be taken as a write-off against ordinary income. However, there's a big loophole in the law, namely an exception that allows most people to write off up to $25,000 in losses from rental income property. The catch is that your ordinary income must be below $150,000 a year to qualify. See the following discussion and consult your tax accountant for details.

:: :: ::

EXAMPLE

Your ordinary income is substantially below $150,000, qualifying you for the exception allowing you to write off loss from investment property. From our example above, you have a $4000 loss (from depreciation) that you can now take as a deduction against your ordinary income (from salary or similar sources). This reduces your ordinary income by $4000 and saves you a substantial amount of income tax that you would otherwise have to pay.

:: :: ::

> **:: HINT ::**
>
> It's worth noting that rental property provides one of the few old-fashioned tax shelters (albeit a modest one) remaining to the middle class. It works in this fashion. When you get a deduction against your ordinary income due to depreciation on real estate, you avoid having to pay taxes at the ordinary income rate. Later on, when that depreciation is recaptured (to be discussed in a later chapter), you pay taxes on it at what may very well be a reduced capital gains tax rate. The difference in rates for ordinary income versus capital gains, is the modest tax shelter.

Can I Take Depreciation Year after Year?

Indeed you can. Depreciation is taken until the property is fully depreciated. For example, if you are on a depreciation schedule lasting roughly 30 years, you would take depreciation each year until at the end of the third decade the property was fully depreciated.

:: :: ::
EXAMPLE

If we assume "straight-line" depreciation, that is, the same amount taken each year, your multiyear depreciation would look something like this.

Original basis $100,000

Depreciation in year 1 .... –$ 4,000

Depreciation in year 2 .... –$ 4,000

Depreciation in year 3 ....–$ 4,000

Depreciation in year 4 ....–$ 4,000

Depreciation in year 5 ....–$ 4,000

Depreciation in year 6 ....–$ 4,000

Depreciation in year 7 ....–$ 4,000

Depreciation in year 8 ....–$ 4,000

Adjusted basis, end of year 8 ....$ 68,000

■ ■ ■

Each year that your depreciation expense contributes to a loss on the property, you may be able to take that loss as a deduction against your ordinary income as described in the preceding text. However, note that each year your basis in the property goes down by the amount of depreciation taken. As a result, the amount of capital gain when you sell will increase.

■ ■ ■

EXAMPLE

Your original basis in the property is $100,000. After eight years it has been lowered to $68,000, as in our example above. At that time you sell for $120,000. What is your capital gain?

Answer: Your capital gain is $52,000—$20,000 is due to price appreciation, $32,000 is due to depreciation taken.

Sales price $120,000

Less adjusted basis ....$ 68,000

Capital gain ....$ 52,000

Sales price $120,000

Original basis $100,000

Capital gain from appreciation ...... $ 20,000

Original basis $100,000

Adjusted basis .... $ 68,000

Capital gain from depreciation ...... $ 32,000

≈ ≈ ≈

As we'll see in a later chapter, the capital gains tax rate is significantly higher for gains due to depreciation than it is for gains due to appreciation. Hence, keeping accurate track of the depreciation taken on a property is now a vital part of your tax preparation process.

≈ TAX PLANNING ≈

If you are in the lowest tax bracket, you want to avoid lowering your tax basis due to depreciation, when possible, in order to avoid paying a higher capital gains tax rate on sale.

In the higher tax brackets, even the 25 percent maximum for recapture of depreciation is an advantage over the 28 to 39.6 percent you'd otherwise pay in ordinary income tax.

Do I Change My Basis When I Refinance My Property?

Refinancing property normally has no effect whatsoever on your tax basis. Contrary to popular belief, refinancing your property does not change its tax status — a new loan does not raise or lower the basis.

☷ TAX PLANNING ☷

Remember that any dollars saved by legally avoiding paying taxes today are worth more than the inflation-reduced value of dollars paid in taxes tomorrow.

☷ ☷ ☷

EXAMPLE

Let's say you buy a property for $50,000, putting $5,000 down and getting a $45,000 mortgage. After costs, your tax basis is $55,000. Subsequently, the value of your property appreciates to $100,000. You decide to cash in on some of your new equity. You're able to get a new mortgage for $80,000, netting you $35,000 (remember, your old mortgage was for $45,000), not counting the costs of obtaining the financing.

Your basis, however, does not move up, even though you now owe $80,000 on the property. It remains at $55,000, unaffected by the refinance. Further, there is no tax of any kind to pay on the money you took out of the property at the time you refinanced.

Original basis $55,000

New mortgage $80,000

Adjusted basis $55,000

☷ ☷ ☷

> ## ⁑ TAX PLANNER ⁑
>
> The dark side of all this is that there will be a capital gain when you sell the property. Yet, because you've already taken money out by means of the mortgage, you may not have the money in the property to pay the tax! You must be careful when refinancing. The money you get may not have tax owed on it at the time of the loan, but tax may be due on it when you sell.

What's My Basis When I Inherit or Receive Property as a Gift?

Generally speaking, when you inherit a piece of property, you get a "stepped-up" basis. That means that the basis becomes the fair market value at the time of the donor's death, regardless of what the basis was before.

⁑ ⁑ ⁑

EXAMPLE

Your parents die in a car accident and you inherit their house. Their old basis in the property (what they paid for it plus costs plus improvements over the years) is $50,000. But the fair market value at the time of the their death is $150,000. What is your basis?

Answer: Your basis is $150,000. You inherit the property, but not the decedent's basis in it.

⁑ ⁑ ⁑

On the other hand, if you receive property as a gift, your basis is usually the lower of either the fair market value at the time you received it or the donor's basis. In other words, if it's a gift, you get the property plus the donor's basis, unless the fair market value happens to be less. (Then a complex set of rules apply; see your accountant.)

✸ HINT ✸

It is usually better to give cash than appreciated assets.

✸ ✸ ✸

EXAMPLE

Property value ... $150,000

Donor's basis   .... $ 50,000 (Because it's lower, this is usually your basis in the property)

✸ ✸ ✸

Should I Calculate the Basis of My Own Property?

As you can see, determining the basis of your property, particularly at the time you sell it, is a precise, technical manipulation, particularly when depreciation schedules are added. If you feel uncomfortable performing this calculation or are inexperienced in tax accounting, you would be wise to secure the services of a CPA or other tax specialist to make the determination for you.

However, once you determine the tax basis in your property, it's relatively easy to determine the capital gain, although you may still want a professional to make the calculation for you. Your capital gain is the difference between your basis and your sales price less costs of sale.

What Are My Additional Selling Costs?

Once you know the tax basis of your property, you are halfway home to determining your capital gain. The other item you need to know is the selling price less the cost of sale. Generally speaking, most of your sales costs can be used to reduce your sales price, with certain important exceptions.

You can normally deduct

- Broker's fees
- Preparation of documents
- Title insurance
- Escrow charges
- Advertising
- Legal fees

As noted earlier, you cannot deduct charges that are ongoing. (If the property is a principal residence, you cannot deduct many charges that would be deductible if it were a rental property, such as fire insurance).

⠸ TAX PLANNER ⠸

There are a number of items that may or may not be included in the costs of sale that we have skimmed over here, including the cost of fixing up the property for sale. A lot will depend on whether it's a rental property or your home. It is beyond the scope of this book to go into the details here. If you have questions, look into a good tax preparation guide book or see your accountant.

How Do I Calculate My Capital Gain?

Finally, once you know your tax basis, your sales price, and your costs of sale, you can figure out what your capital gain on the sale of the property will be.

Capital gain is the sales price less the costs of sale less the tax basis. The formula is

Sales price – Costs of sale – Tax basis = Capital gain

EXAMPLE

You sold your rental house for $150,000 and your costs of sale were $7,500. Your tax basis was $75,000. What is your capital gain?

Sales price	$150,000
Minus costs of sale	$ 7,500
Minus tax basis	$ 75,000
Capital gain	$ 67,500

In this chapter we have learned how to calculate the capital gain on a property. Once we know the gain, we are ready to calculate the tax on it under the new rules. We'll do that in the next chapters.

CHAPTER NINE

Recapture of Depreciation

THERE WAS MUCH concern in Congress that a reduction in the capital gains tax law would create a new tax shelter opportunity for many investors. Congress made great efforts to eliminate most real estate tax shelters in the 1986 Tax Reform Act. Apparently, in the most recent bill, it did not want to give back what it had earlier taken away.

Therefore, Congress included and the President signed a special provision that states that the portion of the capital gain that is due to depreciation will be taxed at a higher rate of 25 percent. Technically, this is called *recapture of depreciation.*

The entire topic of recapture of depreciation is one of the most complex in the entire tax code. The following discussion should, therefore, only be considered an overview. Unless you are very savvy in tax matters, when it's time to sell your own investment property and determine what portion of a capital gain is due to recapture of depreciation, it is suggested that you consult with a tax professional.

How Does Recapture Work?

As noted earlier, most investment real estate is depreciated. This means that each year a certain portion of the value of the property is lost. As it ages, it depreciates in value.

:: HINT ::

It is only possible to depreciate the improvements to property (the buildings). It is not possible to depreciate the land itself. Presumably the land does not lose value through the aging process.

For tax accounting purposes, each year the property owner claims a portion of the depreciation as an expense. For example, the depreciation on your property in a given year might be $4000. You would then combine that $4000 with other expenses including mortgage interest, taxes, maintenance and repair, insurance, and so on. All of these expenses, when combined, would be offset by income from rent to determine whether you had an annual profit or loss.

::: ::: :::

EXAMPLE

Profit/Loss of an Investment Property

Income:	Rents		$19,000
Expenses:	Mortgage interest	$12,000	
	Property taxes	$ 4,000	
	Insurance	$ 1,200	
	Maintenance	$ 1,100	
	Advertising	$ 100	

Repairs	$ 600	
Depreciation	$ 4,000	
Total	$23,000	−$23,000
Loss		$ 4,000

Note that without the inclusion of depreciation there would have been a breakeven in this example. With depreciation there is a $4000 "paper" loss.

❖ ❖ ❖

❖ HINT ❖

Only investment real estate is depreciated. This includes residential rentals, commercial buildings, and virtually any property that is held for profit. Specifically excluded are your residences. You do not, for example, depreciate your home.

How Much Depreciation Do I Take Each Year?

The amount of depreciation taken is determined by the method and term. In recent years investors have been taking straight-line depreciation—an equal amount each year. In past years, highly accelerated depreciation was possible. In an accelerated method, the depreciation rate is increased dramatically: for example, to 150 percent (at one time as much as 200 percent) of straight-line depreciation. The higher the rate, the more depreciation that can be taken annually.

> ## ⚹ HINT ⚹
>
> The current method allowed for depreciating property is the straight-line method—an equal amount taken each year. Currently the term allowed is 27.5 years for rental property and 39 years for nonresidential real property.

The term also has an effect on the depreciation. The shorter the term, the greater the annual depreciation. At one time terms as short as 20 years or less were allowable. More recently, terms of 27.5 years for some types of real estate have been used.

> ## ⚹ HINT ⚹
>
> If you already own property, chances are your depreciation method has already been determined by you or your accountant. Usually you cannot change the term or the method once it is established unless there was an error. If an incorrect life was determined, the IRS has established a fairly easy method to allow changes—check with your accountant.

How Does Depreciation Come Back to Me?

Under the new tax rules, much of the depreciation that is subject to capital gains treatment you've already claimed while you owned the property may come back to you (be *recaptured*) at the time you sell, because a special capital gains tax rate of 25 percent applies to it. This is higher than the top capital gains rate of 20 percent on appreciated capital gains.

Top appreciated capital gain   20%
Depreciated capital gain   25%

For most properties that sell at a profit, the actual capital gains tax rate that you pay, therefore, is likely going to be a blend between the appreciated and depreciated rates.

:: HINT ::

Beware of the confusion over the term *recapture*. Technically speaking, the writers of the new tax law may have used it incorrectly. Consider the following discussion, but keep in mind that we're speaking of one of the most obscure areas of taxation. If the following brief explanation isn't clear, don't feel bad. Most people don't understand this area—get a good CPA or accountant to help you.

Historically speaking, *recapture* refers to a specific type of depreciation. For example, in the past, it was possible for an investor to take depreciation on a property at an accelerated rate. *Accelerated* simply means that more depreciation was taken each year than would be allowed by the straight-line method. (The straight-line method, you'll recall, is dividing the total number of years into the total amount of depreciation and taking equal amounts each year.) An investor who took 150 percent accelerated depreciation took 50 percent more than straight line in the first year.

Later on, when the property sold, that amount of depreciation that was previously taken that was due to the accelerated method (the amount *more* than straight line) was "recaptured" as ordinary income.

(continued)

(*continued*)

(The actual calculation is frighteningly complex and far beyond the scope of this book.) In other words, a portion of depreciation usually attributable to the accelerated method was recaptured at ordinary income rates, not capital gain rates.

Of course, there was that portion of depreciation that was subject to capital gains taxation—that amount attributed to the straight-line method. Thus, in the past, "recapture" meant paying ordinary income tax rates on depreciation not subject to capital gains rates.

If you're straight on this thus far, get ready for the twist. Under the new tax rules, "recaptured" depreciation refers to that portion that under the old rules was nonrecapturable, that is to say, was subject to capital gains treatment at the old up to 28 percent rate. That portion of depreciation that was recapturable under the old law is apparently still recapturable and is still taxed at ordinary income rates.

Got it?!

To be more precise, the new law's recapture rules only refer to that portion of depreciation that would be subject to the old 28 percent capital gains tax rate.

Thus, if you've owned property for a long period of time and once used an accelerated depreciation method, you may find that when you sell you may have to recapture one type of depreciation at ordinary rates and another type at the new 25 percent rate.

As I said, see a good tax specialist!

How Do I Know How Much Depreciation I've Taken?

You or your accountant should be keeping a running total of depreciation taken during the ownership of the property. Further, you'll recall from Chapter 8 that taking depreciation acts to lower your tax basis. You should be able to determine how much your tax basis has been adjusted downward because of depreciation since you originally purchased the property and how much depreciation, if any, will be added back at the time of sale.

EXAMPLE

You make $55,000 a year in regular income and are in the 28 percent tax bracket. You purchase a rental house and keep it for 15 years. The house (not the land) was valued at $150,000 and you depreciated it using a straight-line method over 27.5 years. That means you took an equal amount out ($5455) each year. Each year your loss on the property was at least $5455, which you took as a write-off against your ordinary income. After year 15 you will have depreciated the house a total of $81,818 and your tax basis will have been reduced by that amount. You sell and realize a capital gain of $200,000. What tax rate must you pay?

Answer: You are in the 28 percent tax bracket, so the first $81,818 of the capital gain is considered recaptured depreciation and you would pay a 25 percent rate on it. The remaining portion of the gain ($118,182) is considered due to appreciation and the 20 percent rate applies.

Capital Gain Tax Rate Division

Recaptured depreciation @ 25%	$81,818
Appreciated gain @ 20%	$118,182
Total capital gain	$200,000

‡ ‡ ‡

---

‡ HINT ‡

Sometimes a more graphic representation is easier to visualize. Consider the following "above and below the line" illustration.

Original basis $\dfrac{\text{Depreciation @25 percent}}{\text{Appreciation @20 percent}}$

What if I'm in a Lower Tax Bracket?

If you are in the 15 percent tax bracket and you have depreciation, when you sell there is a distinct possibility you will be paying three separate capital gains tax rates — 10, 20, and 25 percent.

‡ ‡ ‡

EXAMPLE

Taking our previous example, here's how the total tax for the year (assuming 1997 rates) would work out.

	Income	Tax	Table
Regular income	$ 55,000	$10,044	
Depreciation recapture	$ 81,818	$20,455	25%
Appreciation	$118,182	$23,637	20%
Total	$255,000	$54,136	

How does this tax of $54,136 compare to the tax you would otherwise pay if it weren't for capital gains?

Answer: Without the capital gains tax advantage, your tax would be $75,869, over $20,000 more!

Note: Once again it's worth advising that the actual calculations are somewhat complicated and that you should see an accountant about your own tax situation.

∺ HINT ∺

In the past, most investors would try to maximize their depreciation in order to obtain a big write-off against their ordinary income. This took two courses. First, investors would often try to characterize a larger percentage of the property as an improvement and a smaller percentage as land. Remember, only improvements can be depreciated.

Second, investors would go for the highest depreciation rate/method possible. In the past, that meant they would opt for the accelerated depreciation noted earlier. The higher the rate of depreciation, the greater the annual amount depreciated: as a result, the more loss could be shown each year and the greater the write-off against ordinary income taxes. (See the previous discussion on the recapture of accelerated depreciation.)

However, with the recapture of depreciation that is subject to capital gains now at a higher rate than appreciated capital gains, we may see investors in the lowest tax bracket reverse their thinking and aim for reducing the amount of straight-line depreciation taken annually by characterizing less of the property as "improved."

How Do the Active/Passive Rules Affect Depreciation?

We've touched on these in several places, but a brief explanation here should prove helpful. In 1986 the federal government changed the rules by which an annual loss from real estate could be written off against ordinary income.

Prior to that time, many very large investors would buy large real estate properties and then depreciate them in an accelerated fashion. Because of depreciation, these investors would be able to show such a large loss that in some cases they would be able to write off (offset) their entire ordinary income. With the exception of alternative minimum tax (AMT), they would pay no ordinary income taxes.

This was considered an abuse and the 1986 tax laws changed the nature of real estate investment to prevent it. Basically, real estate was deemed a "passive" investment. Income from ordinary sources such as salary was considered "active." You could not offset a passive loss against active income.

Technically, this meant that regardless of whether or not you actively participated in the rental of your property, since it was automatically deemed passive, if you showed a real estate loss you could no longer write that loss off against your ordinary income, with one exception that we'll cover next. (The loss could, however, be used to offset a gain from other passive income.)

How Come My Accountant Writes Off My Rental Loss against my Income Each Year?

As stated, there was one exception. Taxpayers whose ordinary income was under $150,000, and who actively participated in their investment real estate, could still write off up to $25,000 a year in loss against their ordinary income. (The actual amount available was reduced by 50 cents on the dollar for incomes between $100,000 and $150,000 until at $150,000 you lost the entire benefit.)

What Happens if I Can't Write Off My Loss Each Year?

In actual practice, what often happens with investment real estate is that there is a profit after expenses and income are offset, but before depreciation is taken into account. When depreciation is added into the equation, the profit is often erased. Thus the depreciation acts to reduce or eliminate the annual profit from investment properties that would otherwise be added to an investor's ordinary income. Thus, indirectly, it often still reduces ordinary income for investors in all brackets.

However, higher-income taxpayers who do not qualify for the up to $25,000 exemption discussed earlier and who have properties that show actual losses each year due to depreciation are in a different situation. They are not able to deduct the losses because of the active/passive rules. This disallowed depreciation that is not utilized is called a passive activity loss (PAL).

It's important to understand, however, that PALs are allowed at the time the property is sold (the activity is disposed). Thus, while PALs create ordinary deductions (0–39.6 percent tax rate), the depreciation recapture at the time of sale creates a capital gain (0–25 percent tax rate). This is good for the taxpayer!

Thus the active/passive rules exercise a complicated effect on depreciation. What should be obvious is that this whole area is also very complex. (It is beyond the scope of this book to go into a more detailed explanation. Check with your accountant for more information.)

How Does the Recapture of Depreciation Eliminate a Tax Shelter?

Although this issue is discussed previously and elsewhere in this book within other contexts, it's worth taking a moment to consider how a potential tax shelter would work if depreciation were not taxed at a higher capital gains rate. This helps to understand the motivation behind the higher 25 percent rate that was enacted.

At the most basic level, it comes down to the conversion of ordinary income into capital gain, thereby sheltering (reducing the rate of tax on) a portion of the money. It is best explained by an example.

EXAMPLE

You have a commercial property that you depreciate at a rate of $10,000 a year. All else is equal, meaning that the income you receive from the property is exactly offset by your deductible expenses for mortgage interest, taxes, insurance, maintenance, and so forth. Were it not for the depreciation, you would simply break even.

However, because depreciation is considered an expense for the purpose of calculating income/loss from an investment property, suddenly your break-even property is a big loser, to the tune of $10,000 a year—all from depreciation, all on paper.

Let's further suppose that you make about $125,000 in ordinary income. You are in the 31 percent marginal tax bracket. And you handle the rentals yourself.

Now you have a big write-off coming from your real estate investment loss. You *lost* (on paper) $10,000, all due to depreciation. Since your income is low enough to exclude you from the active/passive rules, you can take that entire $10,000 real estate loss as a deduction against your ordinary income. In the 31 percent tax bracket, this means that you've just saved yourself $3100 you would otherwise have to pay in taxes.

Ordinary income	$125,000
Depreciation loss	$10,000
Income reduced to	$115,000

= Tax savings of $3,100

Not bad. Let's further assume that this continues in the same fashion on a straight-line depreciation (meaning an equal amount is depreciated each year) for 10 years. The total amount of depreciation taken is $100,000. And assuming the property continues to break even and your income remains the same, your total savings in taxes you would otherwise have paid would be $31,000.

Depreciation loss/10 years	$100,000
Tax savings/10 years	$31,000

What happens when you sell?

Answer: When you sell the property, you owe a capital gains tax. The tax basis of your property is lowered by $10,000 each year, so that it is $100,000 lower after 10 years. Let's assume you bought the property for $300,000 and sold it for $500,000.

Ten-Year Assessment of Property

Sales price		$500,000
Original tax basis	$300,000	
Depreciation taken	−$100,000	
Adjusted tax basis		−$200,000
Capital gain		$300,000

In other words, $100,000 of your $300,000 capital gain is due to depreciation. That's the part we're concerned with.

\#\# \#\#

```
::  HINT  ::
```

:: HINT ::

While it may not seem like much in our example, the loss generated by depreciation could have been much, much higher. And it can be used to offset a huge profit from other properties that otherwise would have been realized annually, thus, in effect, sheltering money (by offsetting it) in much higher tax brackets.

With a 25 Percent Recapture Rate

With a 25 percent recapture rate, it works out this way for the investor in the 31 percent tax bracket.

Tax savings/10 years	$31,000
Capital gain tax at 25%	$25,000
Tax shelter	$6,000

Eliminating an even greater potential tax shelter was part of the motivation for the tax writers when they created the 25 percent capital gains tax rate on recapture of depreciation.

(Keep in mind that the present value of $3,100 saved each year for 10 years at 6 percent, if you have put the money in a savings account, is $43,724, which boosts that tax savings to over $18,000! Of course, that interest income is taxable!)

⁘ HINT ⁘

It's important to remember that the shelter is created by the conversion of ordinary income into capital gains — the conversion of income taxed at a higher rate to income taxed at a lower rate. This is possible because, while the property does not decline in actual value, you create a deduction each year due to depreciation.

CHAPTER TEN

—❈—

Trading versus Selling

W HILE THE NEW capital gains tax rate reduction is certainly a strong benefit for real estate investors, the question arises of whether it's a good enough benefit to warrant selling property. In other words, even with the new rate reduction, most investors are going to pay between 20 percent and 25 percent in tax on their capital gain. To put it a different way, they are going to have to give away a fifth to a quarter of that gain in taxes to the government. Given the significant amount here, is it perhaps better to not sell at all? Or is there a different alternative?

Over the past few decades, trading the property has been an alternative to selling outright and paying a capital gains tax. This is technically called a Tax Code Section 1031 "non-recognition of gain" exchange, and more popularly a "tax-free" exchange. Hundreds of thousands of investors have opted to trade for another property instead of selling, and in the process not pay any tax at the time of the transaction.

∷ HINT ∷

What we're talking about here is strictly investment real estate—a rental house, an apartment building, bare land held for profit, a commercial building, a strip shopping center, and so on. We are not talking about a home in which you live, either as a principal or second residence. These properties do not qualify for a "tax-free" exchange as discussed in this chapter (although your main house may qualify for the up to $500,000 exclusion noted in the first section of this book).

In this chapter we're going to examine this alternative and see whether it's still as viable an option as it has been in the past. First we'll examine how it's done; then we'll look at its pros and cons.

What Is a "Tax-Free" Trade?

At the outset, it's important to understand that the term "tax-free" is a misnomer. Rather, what happens is that the taxpayer trades one property for another and transfers the current tax basis into the new property. In the process any capital gain is deferred into the future. Thus it is a tax-deferred exchange similar in concept to the rollover of a principal residence that was eliminated by the new tax bill. The only way in which it's truly "tax free" is that there is no tax to pay immediately at the time of the transaction. But the tax is not forgiven or excluded, merely deferred to a future time.

⠿ HINT ⠿

With the rollover of a principal residence eliminated
by the new tax bill, some high-income taxpayers
may wish to convert their principal residence to a
rental in order to qualify for a "tax-free" exchange.
It's probably safe to assume, however, that the government will be looking more closely at these conversions in the future.

How Does It Work?

The basic concept is quite simple, although the execution is
frequently complex, requiring the skills of a professional real
estate trader and a competent accountant. Here I'll present
an overview. If you are contemplating an actual tax-deferred
exchange, I strongly recommend you contact professionals
in the field to aid you.

At the simplest level, you have a property that you wish to
dispose of. Rather than sell it outright and pay taxes on the
capital gain, you opt to trade it for another property. You find
someone who wants to trade and you swap. Provided certain
strict conditions are met, you don't end up paying any taxes
on the transaction, you get rid of your old property, and you
acquire a new (and presumably better) property.

There are, of course, those strict conditions. They include
the following.

- The property must be of "like kind." That means that you
  must trade for a property that has a use similar to yours.
  In recent years this has come to mean, for example, that if
  you have a rental house, you might trade for an apartment building or a commercial building or even bare
  land—real estate for real estate. You could not, however,

trade for stock, bonds, or rarities. (This might change in the future, as discussed at the end of this chapter.)

- Both properties must be "trade or investment" real estate. In other words, they can't be personal residences. This is sometimes a real problem when property is inherited and was never used for trade or investment.

- Normally, for the trade to be recognized by the IRS as not having any gain, you cannot take any cash ("boot") out of the deal. The transaction might be worth $1 million, but if you get $10,000 in cash out of it (as opposed to just the other property), you are jeopardizing the deferral status of the transaction. (There may be a way around this, as we'll see shortly.)

- When these trades first came into popular use, you had to identify the property you were trading for immediately. However, court cases over the years have increased the amount of time for naming the traded property (and Congress wrote it into the tax code to as long as months after the trade). This is a complicated concept that we'll also go into in more detail shortly.

Where Do I Find a Property to Trade for?

That, of course, is the crux of the problem. In order to pull off a trade, you need to pull together two elements. First, you need to identify a property you wish to acquire. Second, you need to find a buyer for your existing property.

The rub comes from the fact that almost never is the potential buyer of your property the seller of the property you wish to acquire. In other words, finding a person who will trade straight across, their property for yours, is a virtual impossibility. Yes, it does occasionally happen. But so does a lightning strike. Going into a trade you have to assume you won't be able to trade straight across.

That means that you must, in addition to identifying a property you wish to acquire, find a buyer for your existing property. In other words, you must conduct both the equivalent of a purchase and a sale at the same time. The buyer for your property is usually referred to as the *third leg* of the transaction.

I'm sure some readers unfamiliar with trades are beginning to wonder how this all goes together. It's not done with mirrors, but it does require accepting a new concept, so please read closely. Here's how a three-legged (or three-tiered) trade is done.

Step one: You have the buyer of your property buy the property you wish to acquire, instead of yours. Be sure you understand this. Your buyer doesn't buy your property. He or she buys the property you want.

Step two: You now trade across the board for the property you want. Assuming it's done correctly, you end up transferring your basis, and capital gain, to the traded property. And your buyer, of course, ends up with your property. (And the seller of the property you eventually acquire gets a sale, which is what he or she wanted all along!)

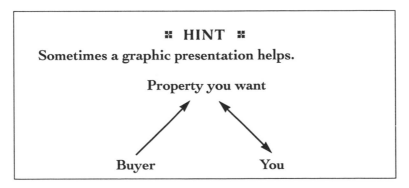

:: HINT ::
Sometimes a graphic presentation helps.

Property you want

Buyer   You

Remember, the reason this works is that the buyer of your property is willing to buy a property you want. This usually presents no problems once the buyer understands how it's all going to work. The seller of the property you want also rarely objects, since he or she is still going to get a cash sale out of the deal.

Perhaps the most difficult part of these transactions is getting everyone to understand completely what's happening. If they are done correctly, the seller and buyer have either no effect or a slight positive tax effect from the transaction. And you, of course, end up with a "tax-free" trade.

What about Cash out of the Deal?

Let's close up a few loose ends. While we've glossed over the surface of this kind of a transaction, keep in mind that there's cash coming in (from the buyer) and going out (to the seller of the property you want). There are typically mortgages acquired and paid off. In short, there's all kinds of money floating around. However, as noted earlier, if you receive any cash out of the deal, it may negate the tax-deferred status of the transaction. But what if you need to get cash out of your existing property for one reason or another?

The most common method of doing this is to refinance your existing property long before the trade. Once your property is refinanced, you have already taken out what cash you need. At the time of the actual exchange, no cash need pass into your hands.

Note: If you do take cash and it doesn't negate the deal, you are only taxed on the gain to the extent of any boot received. The balance of the gain is deferred into the new property.

> ## ∷ HINT ∷
> Another problem is finding a property where the equity is roughly the same as you have in your existing property. This can often be handled by having the buyer obtain new financing on the identified property or having the seller refinance prior to or even during the transaction. (Remember, unless the seller is also going for a "tax-free" trade, he or she should have no problem in getting cash out of the transaction.)

The most difficult problem for most traders, besides finding that buyer for their existing property, is determining what they want to trade into. If you have a rental house, should you trade into another? What about going for an apartment building? Or land? Or a strip shopping center? How do you know you'll be better off after the trade than before? How do you know that the property you're getting will be better than the property you're dumping?

That leads us to the next section: the pros and cons of trading real estate.

The Pros and Cons of Trading

There are usually three reasons an investor will give for trading a piece of property.

1. To avoid paying taxes on the transaction
2. To get out of an existing property
3. To get into a better deal

If all three are realized by the trade, then the investor is a happy person. Indeed, very often trades do work out exactly as planned and there is a decidedly happy ending. However, sometimes they do not.

Will I Get a "Tax-Free" Transaction?

If the deal is structured correctly, you should be able to defer capital gains taxes on the trade. However, you must be sure that the deal works from a tax perspective, and that's typically the job of a well-versed and extremely competent accountant. This is not the time to skimp and do it yourself (unless you've done these before and are very savvy about them). Hire the best—you won't regret it later on.

Will I Get a Better Property?

This is a different matter. Most people who want to trade have strong reasons to get rid of their existing property. Perhaps they can't find good tenants in the market. Or maybe they can't find a buyer. These sorts of reasons are not likely to be mitigated by a trade. If you can't find a good tenant, chances are future owners won't either, and that will reduce your chances of finding a potential buyer (who will probably see the problem you're having). And if you're already having trouble finding a buyer, finding one who'll go along with all the intricacies of a trade may be more difficult, not less.

I suggest that trading is not necessarily a way of getting out of a bad property and into a good one. If this is your motivation, it's often the case that you'll hook up with someone who has a terrible property they want to dump and you'll exchange one bad deal for another, sort of like jumping from the frying pan into the fire.

On the other hand, if your motivation is that you don't want to pay what you consider high capital gains taxes on the sale, then a trade may be for you. You'll change properties and, if the transaction is handled properly, you'll avoid the tax charge, at least for the moment.

Is Trading Better than Biting the Bullet and Paying the Capital Gains Tax?

That, of course, is the crux of the issue. Are you better off doing a tax-deferred exchange or just selling the property and paying the capital gains taxes?

You are certainly better off selling outright with lower capital gains tax rates of today than you were before. Previously, you'd pay up to a maximum capital gains rate of 28 percent. Today, assuming a long-term gain, half recapture of depreciation (assuming it's all straight line—see Chapter 9), and half appreciation, you'll pay at an average rate of around 22 or 23 percent. That's not an insignificant difference. On the other hand, it's not exactly a huge amount of savings either. It still represents giving about a quarter of the gain on the sale to the federal government (not to mention state governments).

I suspect that whether or not to trade will be decided by many investors on the basis of additional issues, such as the following.

- Do I want to continue renting out property or do I want to get out of the game entirely?
- Can I find a suitable property to trade into?
- Am I willing to get involved in a complex transaction?

⚑ HINT ⚑

It is possible to mitigate the complexity of the transaction by hiring an *exchange facilitator*. These are typically real estate agents with accounting and trading backgrounds who can properly structure the deal for you.

For many, after an analysis of the pros and cons of trading, the answer is going to be that it's just simpler and easier to conduct a straight sale and pay the taxes. For others, however, avoiding that tax bite is going to be most important and a trade will be a viable option.

:: HINT ::

Remember that when you do a "tax-free" trade, you don't avoid the taxes forever. You just postpone them. At some point in the future you'll probably sell (assuming you don't trade again) and the deferred capital gain will be taxed. Of course, by then maybe the government will have lowered (or raised!) the capital gains tax rate once more.

Possible Law Changes

It's probably worth noting that the Clinton administration wished to have Congress change the tax code specifically with regard to the definition of "like kind" exchanges. The Administration wanted the language to specify that *like kind* meant exactly what it said. If you had a rental house, you could do a "tax-free" trade for another rental house. If you had an apartment building, you could trade for an apartment building. Bare land for bare land and commercial property for commercial property. But not bare land for a rental house or a commercial building for an apartment building.

This language was not incorporated into the new tax bill. However, things that get proposed once often get passed later on. It's not inconceivable that at some time in the future a new tax bill could change the law, tightening up the definition of *like kind*. And that could severely restrict your options in a trade.

—**▪▪**—

CHAPTER ELEVEN

What if I Can't Cash Out for Enough Money to Pay the Taxes?

W HEN DISCUSSING CAPITAL gains, the assumption always seems to be that there will be enough cash realized from the sale of the property to pay any capital gains taxes. But that may not always be the case. It is not inconceivable that while there may be a substantial capital gain, there may be a very small amount of profit and cash. What do you do when there's not enough cash to pay your capital gain?

There are basically two ways that you can get into the trouble of not having enough money to pay taxes when selling a property: I call them the *refinance trap* and the *depreciation trap*. We'll cover both in this chapter, with suggestions about how to avoid them as well as what to do if you fall into them.

The Refinance Trap

The refinance trap typically hits investors who've owned property for a long period of time. My father, who was a real estate broker for some 30 years, fell into this trap himself. He used to refer to his property as "money trees": He would say, "You buy it, water it, and then harvest it." What he meant by "watering it" was renting it out. "Harvesting" was refinancing to get his money out of the property. He would occasionally refinance properties he owned to get money out.

There's nothing wrong with this. However, when refinancing, it's vitally important that you realize that the refinance itself has no tax consequences, at least not immediately. It doesn't raise or lower your basis. But it does reduce your equity.

EXAMPLE

You buy a four-unit apartment building (four-plex) for $250,000, rent it out, and hold it for five years. During that time your equity increases as you pay down the mortgage and as price appreciation occurs. In year five you decide to refinance and pull $50,000 of equity out of the property. Has any of this affected your tax basis?

Answer: No, not at all. Assuming your original tax basis was $250,000, paying down the mortgage does not lower it. Price appreciation does not raise it. And refinancing has no effect on it. Indeed, you do not report your refinancing or the money you take out to the IRS. (The money you obtain in this fashion is normally yours to spend as you wish.)

Many people, like my father, will refinance their investment properties many times during their tenure of ownership. There are usually no problems, as long as the property remains economically sound and the rental income is high enough to pay the higher mortgage payments of the refinance. Eventually, however, the piper must be paid: that time comes on sale.

The Confusion over Equity

We covered this briefly in Chapter 8, but it's worth going over again. While refinancing has no effect on the tax basis of a property, it does have an effect on what many people consider to be equity. Equity in real estate is defined as the difference between what you owe and what you'd get if you sold the property.

EXAMPLE

You owe $75,000 on a rental house. If you were to sell, you'd get $140,000 after the costs of sale. What is your equity?

Answer: Your equity is what you'd get from the sale less your mortgage. In this case it's $140,000 less $75,000, or $65,000.

The problem is that refinancing reduces your equity. If you take money out of a property by getting a new mortgage, you reduce your equity in that property.

EXAMPLE

In the above example, you refinance and get a new mortgage for $130,000 (including refinance charges). What is your equity now?

Answer: Your equity is sales price after costs minus mortgage—$140,000 less $130,000, or $10,000. By refinancing, you've reduced your equity by $55,000.

Over the years, investors tend to think of their equity in the property as what they pay taxes on. In the previous example, the owners might (erroneously) begin thinking that because they have $10,000 in equity, they'd owe tax on that amount at the time of sale.

However, as we've seen, a capital gain is the difference between the sales price and the adjusted basis. If the adjusted basis is low and the sales price is higher, there can be a substantial capital gain, regardless of the owner's equity in the property.

EXAMPLE

In the previous example, assume that the original basis was $100,000. By the time of sale, it was reduced to $75,000 because of straight-line depreciation. On the other hand, the sales price was $140,000. What was the capital gain?

Answer: The total gain was $65,000. That represents a blend of $25,000 as recapture of depreciation and $40,000 due to appreciation.

EXAMPLE

In the above example, what is the tax on the capital gain?

Answer: Assuming the taxpayer was in the 28 percent or higher tax bracket, The tax on

$25,000 @ 25 percent is $6,250

$40,000 @ 20 percent is $8,000

The total tax on the gain is $14,250.

Following the parameters of the sale as outlined in the previous example, the seller would owe $14,250 in capital gains taxes at the time of the sale. However, the seller would only have $10,000 in equity realized as cash at the time of the sale.

EXAMPLE

Amount of capital gain	$14,250
Amount of equity	$10,000
Shortfall	$4,250

In the above example, the owner would only get $10,000 when the property was sold, but would owe $14,250 in taxes. He or she would have more in taxes owed than in cash received!

∷ HINT ∷

If you have trouble following where the money went, remember the refinancing. The owner kept taking money out of the property and reducing the equity through refinancing. If the property had never been financed (or had only been financed moderately), there would have been plenty of equity left to handle the taxes on sale.

The Depreciation Trap

The preceding example of the refinance has already hinted at the depreciation trap. Here, refinancing isn't the culprit. Rather, the problem comes from simply holding the property for a long time and depreciating it. Depreciation, you'll recall, lowers the tax basis. Over the years the depreciation can add up until, after a great many years, you end up recapturing an enormous amount of that depreciation. At a capital gains tax rate of 25 percent, that depreciation can come back as an enormous amount of cash due on sale.

If you still have a high mortgage and the property does not sell for a great deal more than you paid, you may find that you use up a lot of your cash from the sale paying the capital gains taxes.

EXAMPLE

You own a property long enough to fully depreciate it (straight-line method). Your total depreciation comes to $150,000. You're in the 28 percent tax bracket, and when you sell, all of that depreciation comes back to you at the higher 25 percent capital gains tax rate. What do you owe in taxes on sale due to depreciation?

Answer: **25 percent of $150,000, or $37,500.**

In the above example, chances are that if you owned the property long enough to fully depreciate it, it would have gone up in value sufficiently to yield you enough money to pay your capital gain taxes (unless you had heavily refinanced, as covered earlier).

Nevertheless, a $37,500 tax hit, as shown in the example, is nothing to sneeze at. This is particularly the case if the sellers are seniors intending to use the money from the investment property for retirement or perhaps for nursing care; it can be an enormous problem.

What about Taking an Installment Sale?

In an installment sale, you do not receive all your equity in the form of cash, but instead receive some or all of it in payments over years. If the sale is truly an installment sale, for tax purposes you will basically owe taxes on the money as you receive it.

While an installment sale spreads the hurt around over a period of years, it does not alleviate the problem. Too little equity and too much in taxes remains the problem. (Note: Unless you're very tax savvy, check with your tax professional to determine how to structure an installment sale on your property.)

How Can I Avoid the Traps?

The way to avoid the refinance trap is either not to refinance heavily, or, if you do, to withhold some of the money from the refinance in a separate account that you can later use to pay taxes when the property is sold.

Also, it's important to avoid mistaking your equity in the property for your capital gain. We've seen how capital gain is calculated and how it's different from the way equity is determined. Keep them straight.

The way to avoid the depreciation trap is not to hold properties for very long time periods. This will be discussed in the next chapter.

CHAPTER TWELVE

—❚❚—

Buy/Sell Strategies

ARE THERE ANY loopholes in the new tax law?
This question more than any other seems to keep popping up. Investors wonder whether there are hidden advantages that the capital gains reduction offers, beyond the obvious plus of paying a lower rate.

The answer is that while there may not be any loopholes, there are some interesting strategies that investors can use to maximize profits while minimizing the tax they pay. We'll examine several in this chapter.

The Conversion Strategy

Why pay more taxes if you can pay less? It may seem obvious, but when it comes to real estate it can be a bit tricky. This strategy is quite simple in some respects, a bit complex in others. It goes back to the fact that homeowners, when selling their principal residence, get up to a $500,000 exclusion (discussed in detail in Section I). Investors get no such benefit when they sell their properties. So, why not *convert* an investment property to a principal residence and take advantage of the exclusion?

The concept is quite simple. You own a rental house. When it's time to sell, you'll pay capital gains tax on it. However, before selling it, you convert it to a principal residence (living in it for the qualifying two years). At the time of the sale, you claim the up to $500,000 exclusion, and, assuming your capital gain is less than that amount, pay no taxes.

To good to be true? In a way it is. There are several problems inherent with this strategy. First, you must make the property your principal residence for two years. That means moving in. Many investors aren't going to want to move into their rental units.

Second, there's that depreciation that's been claimed during the tenure of ownership. That has lowered the tax basis and must be dealt with under the new rules. However, beyond these two negatives, this strategy offers many positives.

EXAMPLE

You buy a single-family residence that you rent out for five years. During that time you depreciate it and lower the tax basis $30,000.

Now you convert the property; you move in and use it as your main home for two years. Then you sell. During the seven years you've owned it, the price has gone up considerably. When you sell you realize a capital gain of $275,000. What advantage have you gained by the conversion?

Answer: If you were to sell the property as an investment, under the new rules you would pay tax on the $275,000 capital gain. We'll assume a 25 percent rate on the $30,000 recapture of depreciation ($7,500) and the top 20 percent rate on the balance ($49,000). Your total tax would be $56,500.

However, because you converted to a principal residence, you can take advantage of the up to $500,000 exclusion. This applies only to the portion of the capital gain not due to depreciation. You would still owe $7500 in recapture of depreciation. But you would save a whopping $49,000 in capital gains tax on the appreciation.

It's even better when compared to the old rules. Under the maximum 28 percent previously in effect, you would have owed $77,000 in taxes!

:: :: ::

Is There Anything to Watch Out For?

Yes, the key to the conversion is that it must be for real. You can't play games. You must actually move into the former rental property and use it as your home for the two-year qualifying period. This means doing those things that the IRS is likely to look for as proof of residence, such as having all the utilities (including the phone) in your name, changing your voting location and car registration to the new address, and so forth.

:: HINT ::

The IRS is undoubtedly going to examine such conversions more closely in the future as investors attempt to take advantage of this strategy. Therefore, it makes no sense to attempt to fake a conversion. You must actually move in.

Will This Work for Any Rental Property?

It will work for any residential rental property. It works best if you have a single-family residence that you are renting out. However, if you have a duplex, you can move into one-half of the property. If you have an apartment building, you can move into one unit. Just remember, however, that if the property is part investment, part principal residence, you only get the up to $500,000 exclusion on the part that's your principal residence, not on the part that's rented out. You will have to pay tax on the part that remains a rental investment.

Will This Work for a Second Home?

Yes, it will. Assuming you have a second home that's gone up significantly in value (as have many that are well located at the beach, in the mountains near skiing, and so on), when you sell you don't get the benefits of the up to $500,000 exclusion, because it's a second home.

However, if you convert it to your main home before you sell, as noted above, you can get the benefits. This, of course, takes some planning. You must do the conversion two years in advance and you must actually move in.

------------------------- ⠿ ⠿ ⠿ -------------------------

EXAMPLE

You have a second home, a mountain cabin on a lake, which has jumped up in value. You've never rented it out or taken depreciation on it. If you were to sell you'd realize a $160,000 capital gain. How much can you save by converting it to your main home and living in it for two years before selling?

Answer: If you successfully convert it to your main home, you would pay no taxes at all, since you could exclude all of the gain. Your savings at the top rate of 20 percent would be a sizeable $32,000. (Compared to the pre-1997 Tax Law conditions, the savings would be even more; you would save $44,800.)

\#\# \#\# \#\#

The Serial Purchase/Sale Strategy

If this works once, it should work time and again. And it does. The serial strategy means that you convert a rental to a principal residence once every two years and then sell. This strategy works best for those who already own a number of rental units. If, for example, you own three or four rentals, every two years convert one of them to a principal residence. Live in it for the qualifying period, and then sell. In this manner, with the exception of the recapture of depreciation, you should be able to virtually eliminate the taxes you would otherwise pay.

As noted in Section I, it also works well if you plan to house-hop. You can buy, move in, and then resell a home every two years. Of course, this strategy requires that housing prices go up, and you must choose your locations well.

\# HINT \#

There's nothing written into the new tax law that limits the number of times you can convert rentals into your principal residence, as long as you follow the two-year rule.

The Buy and Hold for a Long Time Strategy

An important rule followed for virtually the entire last half-century by many investors who own real estate has been to buy, rent out, and hold for the future. With the new capital gains tax law changes, however, many investors who have owned real estate for many years are wondering if this strategy still holds water. Is it still a good idea to buy and hold investment property for the long term? Or, as suggested above, do the new tax rules make buying and selling quickly a better option?

Why Buy for the Long Term?

Real estate is a slow-moving investment. As opposed to stocks, where prices can make rapid movements on a daily basis, real estate is far less volatile. A 5 percent or 10 percent price movement in a year is considered large, even during inflationary periods. Five percent up or down on a stock price, by comparison, would be considered mild volatility over the course of a week or even a few days.

⁑ HINT ⁑

The person living in a home approaching $500,000 of appreciation should consider selling, because any gain in excess of the $500,000 is subject to tax. If you sell, you may get the up to $500,000 exclusion.

All of which means that it usually takes time to make money in real estate. Yes, you might have a beach house that suddenly soars in value. On the other hand, you might have an inland rental where prices simply stagnate for years. Generally speaking, with the exception of unstable markets, hot locations, and so-called fixer-uppers, your ability to buy and then quickly resell for a profit in real estate is usually not wonderful. This is normally the case across the spectrum from single-family rentals to apartment buildings to commercial centers. It usually takes time for prices to go up.

⁜ HINT ⁜

The lack of volatility in the market leads to a lack of liquidity. Generally speaking, it is harder to get your cash out of real estate than almost any other investment. You can quickly sell bonds or stocks. Even physical gold and silver are easily disposed of to dealers at the market rate with little inconvenience. To sell a piece of real estate, however, takes much longer. In a good market, it can take several months. In a bad market it can take a year or longer. Of course, you can get at least part of your money out, in some cases, by refinancing. But this has its own carrying costs, which eat into any hoped-for future profit.

Does the Recapture Tax Work against Holding Long Term?

For those in the 28 percent and higher tax bracket, the new rate for recaptured depreciation is 5 percent higher than the top rate for appreciated capital gain. That may not seem like a big difference, but over a number of years it could add up. This brings into question the wisdom of holding for a very long time knowing that when you sell you'll end up paying a higher rate because of the recapture of depreciation. Is the higher recapture rate enough to make holding long-term a poor idea?

EXAMPLE

If your annual depreciation subject to recapture is $10,000 a year, at a 5 percent differential (between the recaptured depreciation capital gains rate and the regular capital gains rate), it is costing you an additional $500 a year in taxes to hold the property.

—————————————— ⠿ ⠿ ⠿ ——————————————

In order to save the 5 percent differential, is it worthwhile to sell the property sooner rather than later? It really comes down to how much profit is made during the time of ownership. If you make more than the 5 percent differential, noted above, by holding the property, then holding makes the most sense. If you don't make more than the differential, however, then holding doesn't make sense.

What about When Compared to Ordinary Tax Rates?

On the other hand, the differential noted above is of little consequence when compared to ordinary income tax rates. The ability to pay a capital gains tax rate of either 20 or 25 percent is a striking advantage when this rate is compared to a depreciation deduction at the ordinary income tax rates in higher brackets of 28 to 39.6 percent. From this perspective, it makes sense to buy and hold for the longer term.

⠂ HINT ⠂

As noted earlier, reducing tax rates always encourages investors to look more closely at economic values. Increasing tax rates tends to warp investments, making investors look less at true economic values and more at tax consequences.

The Good Timing Strategy

It's important to understand that while a property depreciates at a steady annual pace (using the straight-line method), its value rarely goes up steadily. Rather, in most real estate markets prices tend to wax and wane. There may be a period of low or even declining prices (such as most areas experienced in the early 1990s) followed by short periods of wild price appreciation (as occurred in many areas in the late 1980s and mid-1990s).

EXAMPLE

A couple buying a property in Los Angeles in 1987 might have experienced a 20 percent price increase within the first three years of ownership. However, for the next five years after that, they might have experienced a 30 percent price decline, followed by a 10 percent price rise over the next two years. In other words, over a 10-year period the prices might have performed in this fashion:

First 3 years	**Up 20%**
Next 5 years	**Down 30%**
Next 2 years	**Up 10%**

After 10 years, prices could be back where they started (not adjusted for inflation).

Of course, the last 10 years happen to be unusual in that we've seen more price declines in more areas than at any time since the Second World War. Nevertheless, even during this 10-year period, if you bought at just the right time and then sold fairly quickly, you could have experienced *only* price increases (or *only* price declines).

Buying and simply holding during this example period would have netted you a zero price increase. Buying at just the right time, however, and then selling abruptly before prices declined, could have netted a 20 percent or more profit during the same period of time.

The point is that the real estate market usually cares little about tax considerations. The market behaves according to the economic rules of supply and demand.

Therefore, savvy investors looking for profit in real estate must keep their ears tuned both to the pulse of the market and to tax consequences. Yes, these investors are very concerned about whether prices are going up or down. They hope to get into the market in an area and at a time when it's rapidly appreciating. They hope to stay out when prices are stagnant or falling. Yet, they do all of this while trying to take advantage of the various holding periods for capital gains and principal residence exclusion.

How Do I Decide whether to Invest Long or Short Term?

History has shown that if you buy real estate and hold it for the very long term, you will make money almost anywhere in the country. On the other hand, if you buy right and sell quickly, you can make far more money during the same time. (Conversely, if you buy wrong and sell quickly, you can lose a great deal of money.)

A timing strategy in real estate is like timing in stocks, commodities, or any other investment. The investor attempts to identify periods of price appreciation and only buy and sell during those times. The long-term investor will get the benefits simply by enduring. The timing investor, however, profits (or loses) more by quicker moves.

On the other hand, if the investor who moves in and out of the market moves too quickly, he or she runs the risk of paying higher taxes on the profit (midterm gain or ordinary tax rates).

The Fix-up Strategy

The new tax rules are causing rethinking among one group of investors: those who purchase properties to fix them up and resell.

Many times those who fix up property plan to sell as soon after one year as possible. They often need about a year to do the fix-up work; but they also want to limit the amount of interest they must pay on mortgages before selling, so they don't want to go much longer than a year. The old one-year time period for long-term capital gains often tended to fit these needs of fixer-uppers quite conveniently.

However, the new midterm tax treatment has caused some consternation and strategy sessions among these investors. Waiting out an 18-month holding period may just mean more holding costs during the time of ownership, with little in benefits.

❖ HINT ❖

The new midterm capital gains rate (for properties held between 12 and 18 months) is the old up to 28 percent rate. Reread Chapter 7 for details.

The new midterm rate, therefore, has thrown a wrench into the machinery. Should the person rehabilitating a property hold for the additional six months to get a substantially reduced capital gains rate (maximum of 20 percent), or sell quickly, bite the bullet, and pay a bigger tax?

I suspect that now the savvy person working on fixer-uppers will be looking for property that can be at least temporarily rented to offset the holding costs of the longer holding period. Fix it and rent it for awhile before selling, rather than fix it and sell it, may become the rule.

Further, savvy investors in fixer-uppers may also be looking for situations where they can move into the property and extend the rehabilitation period. If they move in, spend two years fixing up the property, and then resell, they may be able to claim the property as their personal residence and avoid paying any capital gains taxes at all!

⚒ WARNING ⚒

To qualify for capital gains treatment, the property really should be rented or become a personal residence (move in while fixing up). If the strategy is to buy, fix up, and quickly resell, there is real doubt that the property would qualify for a capital gains treatment at all (even if the holding periods were observed). The IRS undoubtedly would want to characterize it as a "trade or business" property, like inventory. The seller would end up paying at ordinary income tax rates and might even have to pay self-employment tax!

Will the New Tax Law Change the Way People Buy and Sell Investment Real Estate?

It probably will. As we've seen in this chapter, a new series of strategies, including converting to a principal residence and serial buying and selling, should come into existence.

On the other hand, those who buy and hold for long periods of time will remain, as will the investors who look for opportunities in a hot market by darting in and out.

And of course, there will be the fixer-upper investors who now may be more inclined than ever to move into the property they are working on in order to take advantage of the up to $500,000 exclusion on a principal residence.

SECTION III

Other Related
Tax Law Changes

—❚❚—

CHAPTER THIRTEEN

Taking Money out of an IRA for a First Home

O NE PROVISION OF the Tax Relief Act that has caught the eyes of many taxpayers is a new rule that allows money from an individual retirement account (IRA) to be used toward the purchase of a new home. For those caught between the desire to purchase and the lack of a down payment, this could be a real boon.

However, the new law expanded IRAs into two new categories instead of one with many different options. Before checking out the details of getting the money out for the purchase of a new home, let's briefly review the new IRA options.

> ## :: NOTE ::
> Our purpose here is to discuss the withdrawal of funds from an IRA in order to buy a first home. While, of necessity, some discussion of the IRAs themselves is conducted, it is brief and only summarizes major points. Check with your accountant if you have questions regarding your eligibility to deposit into or withdraw funds from an IRA. Severe penalties could apply in some cases.

The New IRAs

The first IRA we'll consider is similar to that which we currently have. Contributions to the IRA are available to those who don't have a company pension plan. (Under the old rules, if you or your spouse was covered under such a plan, you couldn't make a deduction for the IRA even if you weren't covered. That's been changed so that you can contribute without regard to your spouse's pension status if you otherwise qualify.) The key to this plan is that your contributions are only taxed when you withdraw the money.

Contributions remain at a maximum of $2000 a year. However, the new law increases the number of people who are eligible to contribute by raising income limits over seven years. Currently, deductions for IRA contributions phase out as your income increases to between $40,000 and $50,000 for married taxpayers and between $25,000 and $35,000 for single taxpayers. The new rules increase these amounts to up to $80,000 for married taxpayers and $50,000 for singles by the year 2004.

The new so-called Roth IRA (named after its founder) or IRA Plus works the other way. Here, contributions are not made in pretax dollars. In other words, what you put in is not tax deductible; you must pay tax on it. However, as long you keep the funds in the account for at least five years and wait until the age of 59½, they are generally tax free when removed (including all the interest, dividends, capital gain, and so on they have accumulated).

The eligibility for the Roth IRA is fairly high, between $95,000 and $110,000 for singles and between $150,000 and $160,000 for married couples. The contribution here is also $2000, reduced by deductions you may have made during the year to the other IRA or by your compensation for the year. (You can't contribute more than you make in a year.)

And then there's the old-style existing IRA. This is the one that you may already have. You can, however, decide to roll this over into a Roth IRA. Be aware, though, that there will be tax to pay on the rollover (but no penalty). If a rollover is made before January 1, 1999, the tax on the money may be paid over a four-year period. (Note: there are both income and filing qualifications to the rollover—check with your accountant.) With the Roth IRA, you can continue making contributions after the age of 70½.

How Do I Get the Money out of an IRA for a House?

Under the new rules, you can take money out of a qualifying IRA and not be subject to the 10 percent penalty for early withdrawal, or, in the case of a Roth IRA (where the money has been kept for at least five years), to any tax at all, provided the money is used for the purchase of a first-time home. There are, of course, some limitations.

- The amount is generally limited to $10,000, considered to be over the lifetime of the taxpayer.

- The money must be used for ". . . acquiring, construction or reconstructing a residence." This does, however, include reasonable settlement, financing, or other closing costs.

- You must be a first-time home buyer. While logic would dictate that this means someone who has never before purchased a home, the rules are actually far more lenient. "For the purposes of this withdrawal, the term 'First-Time Homebuyer' means any individual if such individual (and if married, such individual's spouse) did not have present ownership interest in a principal residence during the 2-year period ending on the date of acquisition of the principal residence . . ." (There are also other qualifications with regard to running time limits.)

- It applies to taxable years after December 31, 1997.

What should be obvious is that the rules for qualifying as a first-time home buyer are quite liberal. Also, it may now indeed be possible to withdraw up to $10,000 in many cases for the purpose of buying a home.

EXAMPLE

You've been a tenant for two years, meaning that your principal residence has been an apartment or other location in which you did not have ownership. (You may, of course, own other investment properties—it's just that your main home cannot be owned by you for the qualifying period.) You decide to buy a new home and you need money for the purchase. Can you take cash out of a Roth IRA?

Answer: Yes, but you must qualify. The maximum withdrawal is $10,000. And in order to avoid penalty and taxes on the money withdrawn, it must have been in the account for at least five years.

◼ ◼ ◼

◼ HINT ◼

With a Roth IRA you may also take money out prior to age 59½ if you are disabled, provided you otherwise qualify.

The Bottom Line

The ability to withdraw money from an IRA for the purpose of buying a home is certainly not a panacea. There are limits on the amount of money, on who can qualify, and on whether or not you'll need to pay income taxes on the actual money that is withdrawn. Nevertheless, for some home buyers it can be a new and unexpected source of much-needed funds at a very critical time.

—✥—

CHAPTER FOURTEEN

Increased Estate Tax Exemption

THE TAX RELIEF ACT also provided an increase in the estate and gift tax exemption. While this does not directly affect real estate, it can have an effect on investment property that is part of an estate and as such is briefly covered here.

What Is the Unified Estate and Gift Tax?

As most of us know, there is a death tax in this country. When you die, the government taxes your estate. (That tax, by the way, is very heavy—in some cases it can amount to half or more of the value of the estate after both federal and state government taxes are paid.) However, there is an exemption to the tax, and the government has increased that exemption.

✥ ✥ ✥

EXAMPLE

You have an estate subject to tax at death amounting to $475,000 including stocks, bonds, cash, and real

estate investment property. What are the taxes on your estate?

Answer: Because your estate is less than the exemption, your heirs pay no inheritance taxes. The existing federal exemption is $600,000.

:: :: ::

> ## :: HINT ::
> While it is referred to as a "tax" exemption, the $600,000 (now moving up to $1 million) is not a reduction in the tax, but in the value of that portion of the estate that is exempt.

Beginning in 1998 the exemption increases to $625,000. And it continues to increase (with bigger steps occurring in 2004 and afterward) until in 2007 it reaches $1 million.

> ## :: HINT ::
> The gift tax is calculated into the formula. When an individual receives more than $10,000 a year in a gift from any one person, the excess is deducted from the individual's lifetime unified estate and gift tax exemption.

How Does This Affect Real Estate?

Real estate that is inherited is generally subject to inheritance tax and is taxed at the estate tax rate. Since property values have risen substantially (over the past several decades) in many parts of the country, homes and other investment properties have formed the bulk of many estates. In many cases the combined value of these properties has far exceeded the old $600,000 exemption. The new higher exemption will now make it easier to receive property through inheritance without having to pay heavy federal inheritance taxes.

⁜ HINT ⁜

A spouse owning a home as community property and living in a community property state may not have to pay a death tax on the home on the death of the other spouse. Rather, the community property automatically gets a "stepped-up" basis to current value.

Investors who had previously been concerned about the heavy tax that would be paid by their heirs are now breathing a little bit easier. A greater proportion of their estates will be exempt than ever before, and that amount will increase over the next decade. However, inflation will also increase and the actual amount of the increased exemption in real dollars (adjusted for inflation) may be minimal.

⁜ HINT ⁜

The benefit the government is bestowing is not nearly so great as it might at first seem. It must be remembered that the current $600,000 exemption has not been changed in the last decade of its existence. If we assume a 3 percent rate of inflation, then the original $600,000 exemption adjusted for inflation alone should be over $800,000 by 1997 and over $1 million by the year 2007. The new increased exemption, in effect, is doing nothing more than helping to catch up with inflation.

Is There Anything I Can Do if Property in My Estate Will Be over the Exemption Limits?

There may be, and you should check with a good professional to determine what steps you can take. Generally speaking, those who wish to legally avoid as much of the death tax as possible have in the past used the following methods.

- *Trusts.* This is a complex field; check with your accountant to see what may be available to you.

- *Title.* Changing title to real estate, particularly changing to community property, when possible, could have a beneficial effect.

- *Gift.* Gifting up to $10,000 annually to each heir prior to death is a way of passing the estate on without paying tax.

- *Ownership.* Having heirs put up some of the investment and getting their names on the deed may reduce the amount of future gain that they may have to pay tax on.

:: HINT ::

There is a higher exemption of up to $1.3 million (not to be taken in addition to the unified credit exemption) for family-owned farms and businesses. There are, however, many stringent qualifications, including that the farm or business must be 50 percent of the estate and that the heirs must materially participate for at least 10 years in the business after the death of the decedent. Check with your accountant.

Generally speaking, this is an estate planning issue. While the new tax law certainly helps avoid the death tax, it does not eliminate it for many individuals. Therefore, the best advice is to consult with a professional and come up with the plan, including strategies regarding the ownership and disposition of real estate, that is the most beneficial to your estate.

CHAPTER FIFTEEN

——❖——

The Collectibles and Bullion Connection

I T'S BEEN MY observation that many people who invest in
real estate also invest in collectibles and/or in bullion.
Collectibles include such things as rare paintings and porcelain, antiques, rare coins, rare stamps, and other such items.
Bullion is basically physical gold, silver, platinum, and palladium.

I'm not sure what the connection between real estate and
these items is, except that they are all commodities of a sort.
On the other hand, stocks and bonds tend to be paper wealth,
with nothing you can really touch, feel, or look at. When you
buy real estate, you can see it and touch the doorknob or feel
the dirt run through your fingers. When you buy a painting,
you can hang it in your home and gaze at it in admiration.
When you buy a rare coin or a bullion bar, you can hold it in
your hand and keep it in a collection. But when most people
today buy stock, all they get is a bookkeeping entry. (Fewer
people today actually get their stock certificates, preferring
instead to let the brokerage company hold them.)

In short, what we're dealing with is tangibles versus intan-
gibles. And, as such, what happens with tangibles of all kinds
is likely to be of interest to those who invest in real estate.

Hence this brief discussion on the changes in the new Taxpayer Relief Act of 1997 that affect bullion and collectibles.

⁜ HINT ⁜

This discussion should not in any way be taken to imply that the new tax law allows a tax-deferred exchange (Section 1031) between collectibles (including bullion) and real estate. It does not. For the purposes of a deferred exchange, these remain "*un*like kind."

How Do the New Capital Gains Rules Affect Collectibles?

The new tax law singles out collectibles for special treatment. Unfortunately, this treatment puts collectibles at a disadvantage. Basically the law says that collectibles held for 18 months or longer are subject to the old 28 percent capital gains tax. In other words, they do not qualify for the new top 20 percent or bottom 10 percent capital gains tax. Of course, virtually all other capital items are subject to the new and reduced capital gains tax rate; hence the disadvantage of collectibles.

What Does This Include?

For the purposes of capital gains treatment, this encompasses all collectibles, including the following.

Rare stamps
Antiques of all kinds
Rare porcelain
Rare carpets
Rare paintings
Rare sculptures

Rare coins

All bullion, including gold, silver, platinum, and palladium

Virtually anything else that people consider rare and collect for profit

How Does It Work?

The method of calculating the capital gains tax on these collectibles is exactly as it was before the new tax law was passed. Any capital gain is added to the taxpayer's ordinary income and then taxed at the taxpayer's bracket level or 28 percent, whichever is lower. (See Chapter 8 if you're not sure how this is done.)

What Is the Holding Period?

The holding period is technically 18 months. However, as the tax rate for midterm gain is the same as for long-term gain, when it comes to collectibles, it appears that the effective holding period could be one year. Anything sold in less than 18 months (or perhaps a year) is considered a short-term gain and is added to the taxpayer's ordinary income. (Check with your accountant about time limits.)

It's worth noting that in hot markets, collectibles tend to be bought and sold quickly, often in a matter of weeks or months. In a cold market, however, people may hang onto them for years.

Why Is It a Disadvantage?

The disadvantage comes about from the fact that other investments, including real estate, which is also a tangible investment, now have a much lower long-term capital gains tax rate. Even a real estate capital gain attributable to the recapture of depreciation is taxed at a maximum of 25 percent, 3 percent lower than collectibles. Appreciated real estate has a bottom capital gains tax rate of 10 percent.

What this means is that, faced with the option of buying real estate, collectibles, or intangible investments such as stocks and bonds, many investors will be swayed away from the collectibles and toward the other investments. The new law's disadvantage comes about because it favors other investments by lowering their capital gains tax rate while keeping the rate for collectibles at its old (and, those in the field are arguing, unfair) higher level.

Why Are Collectibles Treated Disadvantageously?

One can only speculate at what may have filled the minds of Congressional law writers when they were considering collectibles. However, for some time there has been an effort to disadvantage collectibles.

My own opinion is that there are those in Congress who feel that the holding of wealth in the form of collectibles is a poor economic choice. When individuals invest in stocks, for example, their capital goes to build companies, which in turn provides jobs and products that grow the overall economy. (Reread Chapter 1 for more information on this topic.) When people invest their funds in real estate, they generally secure a large amount of financing, typically 80 to 90 percent, and this feeds the financial mill of the country, turning money over and producing interest.

However, when people buy collectibles, they generally do it with cash. (This is not so much out of choice as out of necessity—few lenders will provide loans for acquiring collectibles.) And the cash does not go toward helping the economy. Indeed, investing in collectibles is in a sense tantamount to keeping money in a mattress. In effect, it takes money out of circulation. A painting worth $1 million simply hangs on the wall storing that wealth until it is sold, presumably for a greater sum. A rare coin worth $100,000 sits in a collection storing that amount of wealth until it is likewise sold.

Any economy can tolerate a small amount of this. However, back in the late 1970s and early 1980s, when inflation in this country was ripping along at double-digit rates, many people opted for collectibles as a hedge against the devaluation of their currency. So much money was poured into gold coins and stamps and paintings that it began to have a larger economic effect.

Thus, it could be reasoned that the new capital gains treatment of collectibles (actually the retention of the old treatment) is an effort to prevent the purchase of collectibles from having an overly large effect on the economy. It sends a discouraging signal to collectors.

On the other hand, I have spoken with Congressional lobbyists and they argue that there are two other reasons that Congress chose to disadvantage collectibles. The first is that it is difficult to determine collectibles' true value. Get three experts in any field from paintings to rare coins, and each will give a different opinion as to the value of a given item. On the other hand, with stocks or bonds, the value is determined in an open and ongoing market and is quite clear.

I don't believe this argument holds much water. The reason is the comparison to real estate. With real estate, the value is also determined by opinion. Get three appraisers and you're likely to get three different evaluations. Even a skilled property appraiser can only give an educated guess as to true market value. Why is it okay for real estate, therefore, and not for rare coins?

The second reason is the fact that there is no federal regulatory body governing collectibles. The stock, bond, and commodities markets have their federal regulatory boards. Where is the regulatory board to police collectibles?

Again, this argument holds little water in my estimation. After all, where is the federal regulatory board policing real estate? While it is true that each state does have a real estate regulatory board, these mainly control agents and developers, not real estate per se. Once again I must ask, Why is it good for real estate and not for collectibles?

Whatever the reason, the law now disfavors collectibles. That doesn't mean that those making millions buying and selling paintings, antiques, and rare coins are going to be discouraged much from doing so. It just means that others who might have a choice between investments, such as the average person, will look twice before leaping to buy a rare stamp.

How Is Bullion Treated Differently in IRAs?

In the recent past, bullion, with certain exceptions we will note, could not be purchased with money from IRAs. Since a great deal of America's savings is in these accounts ($1.3 trillion at last count), this has put bullion at a disadvantage. In effect, precious metals have been excluded to the detriment of those who are involved in the bullion market. It has also disadvantaged those whose only real savings are the money they put into their IRAs and who want to invest that money in precious metals.

:: HINT ::

The exception to excluding bullion from IRAs has been gold and silver eagles, coins issued by the U.S. government, which were allowed to be purchased by IRAs. These are bullion coins struck by the U.S. mint and sold for a premium over their bullion value by coin dealers and other merchants nationwide.

Under the new rules, Section 304 of the Taxpayer Relief Act broadens the scope of bullion that may be held in IRAs.

Specifically, the new rules allow the following to be placed in such accounts:

"Any gold, silver, platinum or palladium bullion of a fineness equal to or exceeding the minimum fineness that a contract market (meaning the commodities exchange market) requires for metals which may be delivered in satisfaction of a regulated futures contract."

:: HINT ::

We are talking about *physical* metal here. The bullion must be in the physical possession of a trustee of the IRA. We are not talking about a futures contract to buy or sell bullion or an option to buy bullion even though it may have a specific cost and a date.

When Does This Take Effect?

The effective date of the new rule is 1998. It applies to taxable years beginning after December 31, 1997. It does not apply to the 1997 tax year, when the rule was enacted.

What Is Its Actual Effect?

In the past, investors who wanted to put bullion into their IRAs were prevented from doing so, with the exception of gold and silver U.S. eagles as noted above. This meant that those who wanted to invest in bullion were limited to doing so by having their IRAs buy different mining stocks or mutual funds that then invested in mining stocks.

Now, investors apparently can use money from an IRA to purchase Australian platinum koalas; Canadian platinum and gold maple leafs; and bullion coins from countries as diverse as Mexico, England, and China, as long as the coins are up to minimum standards of fineness. Since many bullion coins are already minted at a fineness of around .999, this includes many that have been previously struck.

≈ HINT ≈

It's interesting to note that this new rule comes about just as the U.S. government is about to strike its first platinum eagle coins. Of course, this coin is covered by the new legislation.

It should be noted that the rules do not specifically state that the bullion placed into an IRA must be produced by the U.S. or any other government mint. Rather, it says that ". . . any gold, silver, platinum, or palladium bullion" of a certain fineness may be included. It remains to be seen whether this will be interpreted to include bullion pieces struck by private minters such as Englehard Industries, Johnson Mathey, the Franklin Mint, and others.

≈ HINT ≈

The form the metal takes is not the determining factor; rather, it is the fineness. Bars that meet the fineness requirements are just as suitable as coins, or "rounds" as they are called when issued by private mints.

Should You Put Bullion in Your IRA?

Buying bullion to place in an IRA should be a financial decision. The fact that the new law allows you to do so does not mean it makes good business sense.

Items to consider include the following.

- The potential price appreciation—is bullion going up in value? In recent years, prices have tended either to be static or to actually decline. As with any investment, it does not pay to back a loser.

- The cost of storage—unlike paper investments, it costs money to store bullion. There's typically the cost of a safety deposit box and insurance. These must be weighed against any potential gain from increasing prices.

- Lost interest—money spent purchasing bullion cannot be invested in bonds or even savings accounts. Yet, bullion yields no interest.

Therefore, the interest lost that otherwise would be gained must also be measured against any potential gain from increasing prices.

⁜ HINT ⁜

I've have been asked whether real estate can be included in an IRA. I have not seen it done, but that doesn't necessarily mean it can't. However, rules governing an IRA would probably require that the property be owned free and clear. (If you had a mortgage within an IRA, it might cause part of the income generated by the IRA to be taxable.)

Text of the New Tax Changes

T HE TAX CHANGES with regard to investments is provided to help answer questions the reader may have
that are not covered by the text. In addition to the major provisions, there are 175 "miscellaneous" and "simplification"
provisions that may affect an individual taxpayer. A reading
of these may reveal opportunities or pitfalls, depending on
your individual situation.

Note: the code may be changed by correction bills passed
by Congress by the time you read this.

Title III — Savings and Investment Incentives

Subtitle A — Retirement Savings

SEC. 301. RESTORATION OF IRA DEDUCTION FOR CERTAIN TAXPAYERS.

(a) INCREASE IN INCOME LIMITS APPLICABLE TO ACTIVE
PARTICIPANTS. —

(1) IN GENERAL.—Subparagraph (B) of section 219(g)(3) (relating to applicable dollar amount) is amended to read as follows:

"(B) APPLICABLE DOLLAR AMOUNT.—The term 'applicable dollar amount' means the following:

"(i) In the case of a taxpayer filing a joint return:

"For taxable years beginning in:	The applicable dollar amount is:
1998	$50,000
1999	$51,000
2000	$52,000
2001	$53,000
2002	$54,000
2003	$60,000
2004	$65,000
2005	$70,000
2006	$75,000
2007 and thereafter	$80,000

"(ii) In the case of any other taxpayer (other than a married individual filing a separate return):

"For taxable years beginning in:	The applicable dollar amount is:
1998	$30,000
1999	$31,000
2000	$32,000
2001	$33,000
2002	$34,000
2003	$40,000
2004	$45,000
2005 and thereafter	$50,000

"(iii) In the case of a married individual filing a separate return, zero.".

(2) INCREASE IN PHASE-OUT RANGE FOR JOINT RETURNS.—Clause (ii) of section 219(g)(2)(A) is amended by inserting "($20,000 in the case of a joint return for a taxable year beginning after December 31, 2006)".

(b) LIMITATIONS FOR ACTIVE PARTICIPATION NOT BASED ON SPOUSE'S PARTICIPATION.—Section 219(g) (relating to limitation on deduction for active participants in certain pension plans) is amended—

(1) by striking "or the individual's spouse" in paragraph (1), and

(2) by adding at the end the following new paragraph:

"(7) SPECIAL RULE FOR CERTAIN SPOUSES.—In the case of an individual who is an active participant at no time during any plan year ending with or within the taxable year but whose spouse is an active participant for any part of any such plan year—

"(A) the applicable dollar amount under paragraph (3)(B)(i) with respect to the taxpayer shall be $150,000, and

"(B) the amount applicable under paragraph (2)(A)(ii) shall be $10,000."

(c) EFFECTIVE DATE.—The amendments made by this section shall apply to taxable years beginning after December 31, 1997.

SEC. 302. ESTABLISHMENT OF NONDEDUCTIBLE TAX-FREE INDIVIDUAL RETIREMENT ACCOUNTS.

(a) IN GENERAL.—Subpart A of part I of subchapter D of chapter 1 (relating to pension, profit-sharing, stock bonus plans, etc.) is amended by inserting after section 408 the following new section:

"SEC. 408A. ROTH IRAS.

"(a) GENERAL RULE.—Except as provided in this section, a Roth IRA shall be treated for purposes of this title in the same manner as an individual retirement plan.

"(b) ROTH IRA.—For purposes of this title, the term 'Roth IRA' means an individual retirement plan (as defined in section 7701(a)(37)) which is designated (in such manner as the Secretary may prescribe) at the time of establishment of the plan as a Roth IRA. Such designation shall be made in such manner as the Secretary may prescribe.

"(c) TREATMENT OF CONTRIBUTIONS.—

"(1) NO DEDUCTION ALLOWED.—No deduction shall be allowed under section 219 for a contribution to a Roth IRA.

"(2) CONTRIBUTION LIMIT.—The aggregate amount of contributions for any taxable year to all Roth IRAs maintained for the benefit of an individual shall not exceed the excess (if any) of—

"(A) the maximum amount allowable as a deduction under section 219 with respect to such individual for such taxable year (computed without regard to subsection (d)(1) or (g) of such section), over

"(B) the aggregate amount of contributions for such taxable year to all other individual retirement plans (other than Roth IRAs) maintained for the benefit of the individual.

"(3) LIMITS BASED ON MODIFIED ADJUSTED GROSS INCOME.—

"(A) DOLLAR LIMIT.—The amount determined under paragraph (2) for any taxable year shall be reduced (but not below zero) by the amount which bears the same ratio to such amount as—

"(i) the excess of—

"(I) the taxpayer's adjusted gross income for such taxable year, over

"(II) the applicable dollar amount, bears to

"(ii) $15,000 ($10,000 in the case of a joint return).

The rules of subparagraphs (B) and (C) of section 219(g)(2) shall apply to any reduction under this subparagraph.

"(B) ROLLOVER FROM IRA.—A taxpayer shall not be allowed to make a qualified rollover contribution to a Roth IRA from an individual retirement plan other than a Roth IRA during any taxable year if—

"(i) the taxpayer's adjusted gross income for such taxable year exceeds $100,000, or

"(ii) the taxpayer is a married individual filing a separate return.

"(C) DEFINITIONS.—For purposes of this paragraph—

"(i) adjusted gross income shall be determined in the same manner as under section 219(g)(3), except that any amount included in gross income under subsection (d)(3) shall not be taken into account and the deduction under section 219 shall be taken into account, and

"(ii) the applicable dollar amount is—

"(I) in the case of a taxpayer filing a joint return, $150,000,

"(II) in the case of any other taxpayer (other than a married individual filing a separate return), $95,000, and

"(III) in the case of a married individual filing a separate return, zero.

"(D) MARITAL STATUS.—Section 219(g)(4) shall apply for purposes of this paragraph.

"(4) CONTRIBUTIONS PERMITTED AFTER AGE 70½. —
Contributions to a Roth IRA may be made even after the
individual for whom the account is maintained has
attained age 70½.

"(5) MANDATORY DISTRIBUTION RULES NOT TO APPLY
BEFORE DEATH. — Notwithstanding subsections (a)(6) and
(b)(3) of section 408 (relating to required distributions),
the following provisions shall not apply to any Roth IRA:

"(A) Section 401(a)(9)(A).

"(B) The incidental death benefit requirements of section 401(a).

"(6) ROLLOVER CONTRIBUTIONS. —

"(A) IN GENERAL. — No rollover contribution may be
made to a Roth IRA unless it is a qualified rollover contribution.

"(B) COORDINATION WITH LIMIT. — A qualified
rollover contribution shall not be taken into account for
purposes of paragraph (2).

"(7) TIME WHEN CONTRIBUTIONS MADE. — For purposes
of this section, the rule of section 219(f)(3) shall apply.

"(d) DISTRIBUTION RULES. — For purposes of this title —

"(1) GENERAL RULES. —

"(A) EXCLUSIONS FROM GROSS INCOME. — Any qualified distribution from a Roth IRA shall not be includible
in gross income.

"(B) NONQUALIFIED DISTRIBUTIONS. — In applying
section 72 to any distribution from a Roth IRA which is
not a qualified distribution, such distribution shall be
treated as made from contributions to the Roth IRA to
the extent that such distribution, when added to all previous distributions from the Roth IRA, does not exceed
the aggregate amount of contributions to the Roth IRA.

"(2) QUALIFIED DISTRIBUTION. — For purposes of this
subsection —

"(A) IN GENERAL.—The term 'qualified distribution' means any payment or distribution—

"(i) made on or after the date on which the individual attains age 59½,

"(ii) made to a beneficiary (or to the estate of the individual) on or after the death of the individual,

"(iii) attributable to the individual's being disabled (within the meaning of section 72(m)(7)), or

"(iv) which is a qualified special purpose distribution.

"(B) CERTAIN DISTRIBUTIONS WITHIN 5 YEARS.—A payment or distribution shall not be treated as a qualified distribution under subparagraph (A) if—

"(i) it is made within the 5-taxable year period beginning with the 1st taxable year for which the individual made a contribution to a Roth IRA (or such individual's spouse made a contribution to a Roth IRA) established for such individual, or

"(ii) in the case of a payment or distribution properly allocable (as determined in the manner prescribed by the Secretary) to a qualified rollover contribution from an individual retirement plan other than a Roth IRA (or income allocable thereto), it is made within the 5-taxable year period beginning with the taxable year in which the rollover contribution was made.

"(3) ROLLOVERS FROM AN IRA OTHER THAN A ROTH IRA.—

"(A) IN GENERAL.—Notwithstanding section 408(d)(3), in the case of any distribution to which this paragraph applies—

"(i) there shall be included in gross income any amount which would be includible were it not part of a qualified rollover contribution, "(ii) section 72(t) shall not apply, and

"(iii) in the case of a distribution before January 1, 1999, any amount required to be included in gross income by reason of this paragraph shall be so included ratably over the 4-taxable year period beginning with the taxable year in which the payment or distribution is made.

"(B) DISTRIBUTIONS TO WHICH PARAGRAPH APPLIES. — This paragraph shall apply to a distribution from an individual retirement plan (other than a Roth IRA) maintained for the benefit of an individual which is contributed to a Roth IRA maintained for the benefit of such individual in a qualified rollover contribution.

"(C) CONVERSIONS. — The conversion of an individual retirement plan (other than a Roth IRA) to a Roth IRA shall be treated for purposes of this paragraph as a distribution to which this paragraph applies.

"(D) CONVERSION OF EXCESS CONTRIBUTIONS. — If, no later than the due date for filing the return of tax for any taxable year (without regard to extensions), an individual transfers, from an individual retirement plan (other than a Roth IRA), contributions for such taxable year (and any earnings allocable thereto) to a Roth IRA, no such amount shall be includible in gross income to the extent no deduction was allowed with respect to such amount.

"(E) ADDITIONAL REPORTING REQUIREMENTS. — Trustees of Roth IRAs, trustees of individual retirement plans, or both, whichever is appropriate, shall include such additional information in reports required under section 408(i) as the Secretary may require to ensure that amounts required to be included in gross income under subparagraph (A) are so included.

"(4) COORDINATION WITH INDIVIDUAL RETIREMENT ACCOUNTS. — Section 408(d)(2) shall be applied separately with respect to Roth IRAs and other individual retirement plans.

"(5) QUALIFIED SPECIAL PURPOSE DISTRIBUTION. — For purposes of this section, the term 'qualified special purpose distribution' means any distribution to which subparagraph (F) of section 72(t)(2) applies.

"(e) QUALIFIED ROLLOVER CONTRIBUTION. — For purposes of this section, the term 'qualified rollover contribution' means a rollover contribution to a Roth IRA from another such account, or from an individual retirement plan, but only if such rollover contribution meets the requirements of section 408(d)(3). For purposes of section 408(d)(3)(B), there shall be disregarded any qualified rollover contribution from an individual retirement plan (other than a Roth IRA) to a Roth IRA.".

(b) EXCESS CONTRIBUTIONS. — Section 4973(b), as amended by title II, is amended by adding at the end the following new subsection:

"(f) EXCESS CONTRIBUTIONS TO ROTH IRAS. — For purposes of this section, in the case of contributions to a Roth IRA (within the meaning of section 408A(b)), the term 'excess contributions' means the sum of —

"(1) the excess (if any) of —

"(A) the amount contributed for the taxable year to such accounts (other than a qualified rollover contribution described in section 408A(e)), over

"(B) the amount allowable as a contribution under sections 408A (c)(2) and (c)(3), and

"(2) the amount determined under this subsection for the preceding taxable year, reduced by the sum of —

"(A) the distributions out of the accounts for the taxable year, and

"(B) the excess (if any) of the maximum amount allowable as a contribution under sections 408A (c)(2)

and (c)(3) for the taxable year over the amount contributed to the accounts for the taxable year.
For purposes of this subsection, any contribution which is dis-
tributed from a Roth IRA in a distribution described in section 408(d)(4) shall be treated as an amount not contributed."

(c) SPOUSAL IRA. — Clause (ii) of section 219(c)(1)(B) is
amended to read as follows:

"(ii) the compensation includible in the gross
income of such individual's spouse for the taxable
year reduced by —

"(I) the amount allowed as a deduction under
subsection (a) to such spouse for such taxable year,
and

"(II) the amount of any contribution on behalf of
such spouse to a Roth IRA under section 408A for
such taxable year.".

(d) AUTHORITY TO PRESCRIBE NECESSARY REPORTING. —
Section 408(i) is amended —

(1) by striking "under regulations", and

(2) by striking "in such regulations" each place it appears.

(e) CONFORMING AMENDMENT. — The table of sections for
subpart A of part I of subchapter D of chapter 1 is amended
by inserting after the item relating to section 408 the following new item:

"Sec. 408A. Roth IRAs.".

(f) EFFECTIVE DATE. — The amendments made by this section shall apply to taxable years beginning after December
31, 1997.

SEC. 303. DISTRIBUTIONS FROM CERTAIN PLANS MAY BE USED WITHOUT PENALTY TO PURCHASE FIRST HOMES.

(a) IN GENERAL. — Paragraph (2) of section 72(t) (relating
to exceptions to 10-percent additional tax on early distributions from qualified retirement plans), as amended by section

203, is amended by adding at the end the following new sub-paragraph:

"(F) DISTRIBUTIONS FROM CERTAIN PLANS FOR FIRST HOME PURCHASES. — Distributions to an individual from an individual retirement plan which are qualified first-time homebuyer distributions (as defined in paragraph (8)). Distributions shall not be taken into account under the preceding sentence if such distributions are described in subparagraph (A), (C), (D), or (E) or to the extent paragraph (1) does not apply to such distributions by reason of subparagraph (B).".

(b) DEFINITIONS. — Section 72(t), as amended by section 203, is amended by adding at the end the following new paragraphs:

"(8) QUALIFIED FIRST-TIME HOMEBUYER DISTRIBUTIONS. — For purposes of paragraph (2)(F) —

"(A) IN GENERAL. — The term 'qualified first-time homebuyer distribution' means any payment or distribution received by an individual to the extent such payment or distribution is used by the individual before the close of the 120th day after the day on which such payment or distribution is received to pay qualified acquisition costs with respect to a principal residence of a first-time homebuyer who is such individual, the spouse of such individual, or any child, grandchild, or ancestor of such individual or the individual's spouse.

"(B) LIFETIME DOLLAR LIMITATION. — The aggregate amount of payments or distributions received by an individual which may be treated as qualified first-time homebuyer distributions for any taxable year shall not exceed the excess (if any) of —

"(i) $10,000, over

"(ii) the aggregate amounts treated as qualified first-time homebuyer distributions with respect to such individual for all prior taxable years.

"(C) QUALIFIED ACQUISITION COSTS. — For purposes of this paragraph, the term 'qualified acquisition costs' means the costs of acquiring, constructing, or reconstructing a residence. Such term includes any usual or reasonable settlement, financing, or other closing costs.

"(D) FIRST-TIME HOMEBUYER; OTHER DEFINITIONS. — For purposes of this paragraph —

"(i) FIRST-TIME HOMEBUYER. — The term 'first-time homebuyer' means any individual if —

"(I) such individual (and if married, such individual's spouse) had no present ownership interest in a principal residence during the 2-year period ending on the date of acquisition of the principal residence to which this paragraph applies, and

"(II) subsection (h) or (k) of section 1034 (as in effect on the day before the date of the enactment of this paragraph) did not suspend the running of any period of time specified in section 1034 (as so in effect) with respect to such individual on the day before the date the distribution is applied pursuant to subparagraph (A).

"(ii) PRINCIPAL RESIDENCE. — The term 'principal residence' has the same meaning as when used in section 121.

"(iii) DATE OF ACQUISITION. — The term 'date of acquisition' means the date —

"(I) on which a binding contract to acquire the principal residence to which subparagraph (A) applies is entered into, or

"(II) on which construction or reconstruction of such a principal residence is commenced.

"(E) SPECIAL RULE WHERE DELAY IN ACQUISITION. — If any distribution from any individual retirement plan fails to meet the requirements of subparagraph (A)

solely by reason of a delay or cancellation of the purchase or construction of the residence, the amount of the distribution may be contributed to an individual retirement plan as provided in section 408(d)(3)(A)(i) (determined by substituting '120 days' for '60 days' in such section), except that—

"(i) section 408(d)(3)(B) shall not be applied to such contribution, and

"(ii) such amount shall not be taken into account in determining whether section 408(d)(3)(B) applies to any other amount.".

(c) EFFECTIVE DATE.—The amendments made by this section shall apply to payments and distributions in taxable years beginning after December 31, 1997.

SEC. 304. CERTAIN BULLION NOT TREATED AS COLLECTIBLES.

(a) IN GENERAL.—Paragraph (3) of section 408(m) (relating to exception for certain coins) is amended to read as follows:

"(3) EXCEPTION FOR CERTAIN COINS AND BULLION.— For purposes of this subsection, the term 'collectible' shall not include—

"(A) any coin which is—

"(i) a gold coin described in paragraph (7), (8), (9), or (10) of section 5112(a) of title 31, United States Code,

"(ii) a silver coin described in section 5112(e) of title 31, United States Code,

"(iii) a platinum coin described in section 5112(k) of title 31, United States Code, or

"(iv) a coin issued under the laws of any State, or

"(B) any gold, silver, platinum, or palladium bullion of a fineness equal to or exceeding the minimum fineness that a contract market (as described in section 7 of the Commodity Exchange Act, 7 U.S.C. 7) requires for metals which may be delivered in satisfaction of a regulated futures contract,

if such bullion is in the physical possession of a trustee described under subsection (a) of this section.".

(b) EFFECTIVE DATE. — The amendment made by this section shall apply to taxable years beginning after December 31, 1997.

Subtitle B — Capital Gains

SEC. 311. MAXIMUM CAPITAL GAINS RATES FOR INDIVIDUALS.

(a) IN GENERAL. — Subsection (h) of section 1 (relating to maximum capital gains rate) is amended to read as follows:

"(h) MAXIMUM CAPITAL GAINS RATE. —

"(1) IN GENERAL. — If a taxpayer has a net capital gain for any taxable year, the tax imposed by this section for such taxable year shall not exceed the sum of —

"(A) a tax computed at the rates and in the same manner as if this subsection had not been enacted on the greater of —

"(i) taxable income reduced by the net capital gain, or

"(ii) the lesser of —

"(I) the amount of taxable income taxed at a rate below 28 percent, or

"(II) taxable income reduced by the adjusted net capital gain, plus

"(B) 25 percent of the excess (if any) of —

"(i) the unrecaptured section 1250 gain (or, if less, the net capital gain), over

"(ii) the excess (if any) of —

"(I) the sum of the amount on which tax is determined under subparagraph (A) plus the net capital gain, over

"(II) taxable income, plus

"(C) 28 percent of the amount of taxable income in excess of the sum of—

"(i) the adjusted net capital gain, plus

"(ii) the sum of the amounts on which tax is determined under subparagraphs (A) and (B), plus

"(D) 10 percent of so much of the taxpayer's adjusted net capital gain (or, if less, taxable income) as does not exceed the excess (if any) of—

"(i) the amount of taxable income which would (without regard to this paragraph) be taxed at a rate below 28 percent, over

"(ii) the taxable income reduced by the adjusted net capital gain, plus

"(E) 20 percent of the taxpayer's adjusted net capital gain (or, if less, taxable income) in excess of the amount on which a tax is determined under subparagraph (D).

"(2) REDUCED CAPITAL GAIN RATES FOR QUALIFIED 5-YEAR GAIN. —

"(A) REDUCTION IN 10-PERCENT RATE. — In the case of any taxable year beginning after December 31, 2000, the rate under paragraph (1)(D) shall be 8 percent with respect to so much of the amount to which the 10-percent rate would otherwise apply as does not exceed qualified 5-year gain, and 10 percent with respect to the remainder of such amount.

"(B) REDUCTION IN 20-PERCENT RATE. — The rate under paragraph (1)(E) shall be 18 percent with respect to so much of the amount to which the 20-percent rate would otherwise apply as does not exceed the lesser of—

"(i) the excess of qualified 5-year gain over the amount of such gain taken into account under subparagraph (A) of this paragraph, or

"(ii) the amount of qualified 5-year gain (determined by taking into account only property the holding period for which begins after December 31, 2000),

and 20 percent with respect to the remainder of such amount. For purposes of determining under the preceding sentence whether the holding period of property begins after December 31, 2000, the holding period of property acquired pursuant to the exercise of an option (or other right or obligation to acquire property) shall include the period such option (or other right or obligation) was held.

"(3) NET CAPITAL GAIN TAKEN INTO ACCOUNT AS INVESTMENT INCOME. — For purposes of this subsection, the net capital gain for any taxable year shall be reduced (but not below zero) by the amount which the taxpayer takes into account as investment income under section 163(d)(4)(B)(iii).

"(4) ADJUSTED NET CAPITAL GAIN. — For purposes of this subsection, the term 'adjusted net capital gain' means net capital gain determined without regard to—

"(A) collectibles gain,

"(B) unrecaptured section 1250 gain,

"(C) section 1202 gain, and

"(D) mid-term gain.

"(5) COLLECTIBLES GAIN. — For purposes of this subsection—

"(A) IN GENERAL. — The term 'collectibles gain' means gain from the sale or exchange of a collectible (as defined in section 408(m) without regard to paragraph (3) thereof) which is a capital asset held for more than 1 year but only to the extent such gain is taken into account in computing gross income.

"(B) PARTNERSHIPS, ETC.—For purposes of subparagraph (A), any gain from the sale of an interest in a partnership, S corporation, or trust which is attributable to unrealized appreciation in the value of collectibles shall be treated as gain from the sale or exchange of a collectible. Rules similar to the rules of section 751 shall apply for purposes of the preceding sentence.

"(6) UNRECAPTURED SECTION 1250 GAIN.—For purposes of this subsection—

"(A) IN GENERAL.—The term 'unrecaptured section 1250 gain' means the amount of long-term capital gain which would be treated as ordinary income if—

"(i) section 1250(b)(1) included all depreciation and the applicable percentage under section 1250(a) were 100 percent, and

"(ii) in the case of gain properly taken into account after July 28, 1997, only gain from section 1250 property held for more than 18 months were taken into account.

"(B) LIMITATION WITH RESPECT TO SECTION 1231 PROPERTY.—The amount of unrecaptured section 1250 gain from sales, exchanges, and conversions described in section 1231(a)(3)(A) for any taxable year shall not exceed the excess of the net section 1231 gain (as defined in section 1231(c)(3)) for such year over the amount treated as ordinary income under section 1231(c)(1) for such year.

"(C) PRE-MAY 7, 1997, GAIN.—In the case of a taxable year which includes May 7, 1997, subparagraph (A) shall be applied by taking into account only the gain properly taken into account for the portion of the taxable year after May 6, 1997.

"(7) SECTION 1202 GAIN.—For purposes of this subsection, the term 'section 1202 gain' means an amount equal to the gain excluded from gross income under section 1202(a).

"(8) MID-TERM GAIN.—For purposes of this subsection, the term 'mid-term gain' means the amount which would be adjusted net capital gain for the taxable year if—

"(A) adjusted net capital gain were determined by taking into account only the gain or loss properly taken into account after July 28, 1997, from property held for more than 1 year but not more than 18 months, and

"(B) paragraph (3) and section 1212 did not apply.

"(9) QUALIFIED 5-YEAR GAIN.—For purposes of this subsection, the term 'qualified 5-year gain' means the amount of long-term capital gain which would be computed for the taxable year if only gains from the sale or exchange of property held by the taxpayer for more than 5 years were taken into account. The determination under the preceding sentence shall be made without regard to collectibles gain, unrecaptured section 1250 gain (determined without regard to subparagraph (B) of paragraph (6)), section 1202 gain, or mid-term gain.

"(10) PRE-EFFECTIVE DATE GAIN.—

"(A) IN GENERAL.—In the case of a taxable year which includes May 7, 1997, gains and losses properly taken into account for the portion of the taxable year before May 7, 1997, shall be taken into account in determining mid-term gain as if such gains and losses were described in paragraph (8)(A).

"(B) SPECIAL RULES FOR PASS-THRU ENTITIES.—In applying subparagraph (A) with respect to any pass-thru entity, the determination of when gains and loss are properly taken into account shall be made at the entity level.

"(C) PASS-THRU ENTITY DEFINED. — For purposes of subparagraph (B), the term 'pass-thru entity' means—

"(i) a regulated investment company,

"(ii) a real estate investment trust,

"(iii) an S corporation,

"(iv) a partnership,

"(v) an estate or trust, and

"(vi) a common trust fund.

"(11) TREATMENT OF PASS-THRU ENTITIES. — The Secretary may prescribe such regulations as are appropriate (including regulations requiring reporting) to apply this subsection in the case of sales and exchanges by pass-thru entities (as defined in paragraph (10)(C)) and of interests in such entities.". (b) MINIMUM TAX. —

(1) IN GENERAL. — Subsection (b) of section 55 is amended by adding at the end the following new paragraph:

"(3) MAXIMUM RATE OF TAX ON NET CAPITAL GAIN OF NONCORPORATE TAXPAYERS. — The amount determined under the first sentence of paragraph (1)(A)(i) shall not exceed the sum of—

"(A) the amount determined under such first sentence computed at the rates and in the same manner as if this paragraph had not been enacted on the taxable excess reduced by the lesser of—

"(i) the net capital gain, or

"(ii) the sum of—

"(I) the adjusted net capital gain, plus

"(II) the unrecaptured section 1250 gain, plus

"(B) 25 percent of the lesser of—

"(i) the unrecaptured section 1250 gain, or

"(ii) the amount of taxable excess in excess of the sum of—

"(I) the adjusted net capital gain, plus

"(II) the amount on which a tax is determined under subparagraph (A), plus

"(C) 10 percent of so much of the taxpayer's adjusted net capital gain (or, if less, taxable excess) as does not exceed the amount on which a tax is determined under section 1(h)(1)(D), plus

"(D) 20 percent of the taxpayer's adjusted net capital gain (or, if less, taxable excess) in excess of the amount on which tax is determined under subparagraph (C).

In the case of taxable years beginning after December 31, 2000, rules similar to the rules of section 1(h)(2) shall apply for purposes of subparagraphs (C) and (D). Terms used in this paragraph which are also used in section 1(h) shall have the respective meanings given such terms by section 1(h).".

(2) CONFORMING AMENDMENTS. —

(A) Clause (ii) of section 55(b)(1)(A) is amended by striking "clause (i)" and inserting "this subsection".

(B) Paragraph (7) of section 57(a) is amended by striking "one-half" and inserting "42 percent".

(c) OTHER CONFORMING AMENDMENTS. —

(1) Paragraph (1) of section 1445(e) is amended by striking "28 percent" and inserting "20 percent".

(2) The second sentence of section 7518(g)(6)(A), and the second sentence of section 607(h)(6)(A) of the Merchant Marine Act, 1936, are each amended by striking "28 percent" and inserting "20 percent".

(3) Paragraph (2) of section 904(b) is amended by adding at the end the following new subparagraph:

"(C) COORDINATION WITH CAPITAL GAINS RATES. — The Secretary may by regulations modify the application of this paragraph and paragraph (3) to the extent necessary to properly reflect any capital gain rate differential under section 1(h) or 1201(a) and the computation of net capital gain.".

(d) EFFECTIVE DATES.—

(1) IN GENERAL.—Except as provided in paragraph (2), the amendments made by this section shall apply to taxable years ending after May 6, 1997.

(2) WITHHOLDING.—The amendment made by subsection (c)(1) shall apply only to amounts paid after the date of the enactment of this Act.

(e) ELECTION TO RECOGNIZE GAIN ON ASSETS HELD ON JANUARY 1, 2001.—For purposes of the Internal Revenue Code of 1986—

(1) IN GENERAL.—A taxpayer other than a corporation may elect to treat—

(A) any readily tradable stock (which is a capital asset) held by such taxpayer on January 1, 2001, and not sold before the next business day after such date, as having been sold on such next business day for an amount equal to its closing market price on such next business day (and as having been reacquired on such next business day for an amount equal to such closing market price), and

(B) any other capital asset or property used in the trade or business (as defined in section 1231(b) of the Internal Revenue Code of 1986) held by the taxpayer on January 1, 2001, as having been sold on such date for an amount equal to its fair market value on such date (and as having been reacquired on such date for an amount equal to such fair market value).

(2) TREATMENT OF GAIN OR LOSS.—

(A) Any gain resulting from an election under paragraph (1) shall be treated as received or accrued on the date the asset is treated as sold under paragraph (1) and shall be recognized notwithstanding any provision of the Internal Revenue Code of 1986.

(B) Any loss resulting from an election under paragraph (1) shall not be allowed for any taxable year.

(3) ELECTION.—An election under paragraph (1) shall be made in such manner as the Secretary of the Treasury or his delegate may prescribe and shall specify the assets for which such election is made. Such an election, once made with respect to any asset, shall be irrevocable.

(4) READILY TRADABLE STOCK.—For purposes of this subsection, the term "readily tradable stock" means any stock which, as of January 1, 2001, is readily tradable on an established securities market or otherwise.

SEC. 312. EXEMPTION FROM TAX FOR GAIN ON SALE OF PRINCIPAL RESIDENCE.

(a) IN GENERAL.—Section 121 (relating to one-time exclusion of gain from sale of principal residence by individual who has attained age 55) is amended to read as follows:

"SEC. 121. EXCLUSION OF GAIN FROM SALE OF PRINCIPAL RESIDENCE.

"(a) EXCLUSION.—Gross income shall not include gain from the sale or exchange of property if, during the 5-year period ending on the date of the sale or exchange, such property has been owned and used by the taxpayer as the taxpayer's principal residence for periods aggregating 2 years or more.

"(b) LIMITATIONS.—

"(1) IN GENERAL.—The amount of gain excluded from gross income under subsection (a) with respect to any sale or exchange shall not exceed $250,000.

"(2) $500,000 LIMITATION FOR CERTAIN JOINT RETURNS.—Paragraph (1) shall be applied by substituting '$500,000' for '$250,000' if—

"(A) a husband and wife make a joint return for the taxable year of the sale or exchange of the property,

"(B) either spouse meets the ownership requirements of subsection (a) with respect to such property,

"(C) both spouses meet the use requirements of subsection (a) with respect to such property, and

"(D) neither spouse is ineligible for the benefits of subsection (a) with respect to such property by reason of paragraph (3).

"(3) APPLICATION TO ONLY 1 SALE OR EXCHANGE EVERY 2 YEARS. —

"(A) IN GENERAL. —Subsection (a) shall not apply to any sale or exchange by the taxpayer if, during the 2-year period ending on the date of such sale or exchange, there was any other sale or exchange by the taxpayer to which subsection (a) applied.

"(B) PRE-MAY 7, 1997, SALES NOT TAKEN INTO ACCOUNT. —Subparagraph (Λ) shall be applied without regard to any sale or exchange before May 7, 1997.

"(c) EXCLUSION FOR TAXPAYERS FAILING TO MEET CERTAIN REQUIREMENTS. —

"(1) IN GENERAL. — In the case of a sale or exchange to which this subsection applies, the ownership and use requirements of subsection (a) shall not apply and subsection (b)(3) shall not apply; but the amount of gain excluded from gross income under subsection (a) with respect to such sale or exchange shall not exceed—

"(A) the amount which bears the same ratio to the amount which would be so excluded under this section if such requirements had been met, as

"(B) the shorter of—

"(i) the aggregate periods, during the 5-year period ending on the date of such sale or exchange, such property has been owned and used by the taxpayer as the taxpayer's principal residence, or

"(ii) the period after the date of the most recent

prior sale or exchange by the taxpayer to which subsection (a) applied and before the date of such sale or exchange,

bears to 2 years.

"(2) SALES AND EXCHANGES TO WHICH SUBSECTION APPLIES.—This subsection shall apply to any sale or exchange if—

"(A) subsection (a) would not (but for this subsection) apply to such sale or exchange by reason of—

"(i) a failure to meet the ownership and use requirements of subsection (a), or

"(ii) subsection (b)(3), and

"(B) such sale or exchange is by reason of a change in place of employment, health, or, to the extent provided in regulations, unforeseen circumstances.

"(d) SPECIAL RULES.—

"(1) JOINT RETURNS.—If a husband and wife make a joint return for the taxable year of the sale or exchange of the property, subsections (a) and (c) shall apply if either spouse meets the ownership and use requirements of subsection (a) with respect to such property.

"(2) PROPERTY OF DECEASED SPOUSE.—For purposes of this section, in the case of an unmarried individual whose spouse is deceased on the date of the sale or exchange of property, the period such unmarried individual owned and used such property shall include the period such deceased spouse owned and used such property before death.

"(3) PROPERTY OWNED BY SPOUSE OR FORMER SPOUSE.—For purposes of this section—

"(A) PROPERTY TRANSFERRED TO INDIVIDUAL FROM SPOUSE OR FORMER SPOUSE.—In the case of an individual holding property transferred to such individual in a transaction described in section 1041(a), the period such individual owns such property shall include the period the transferor owned the property.

"(B) PROPERTY USED BY FORMER SPOUSE PURSUANT TO DIVORCE DECREE, ETC. — Solely for purposes of this section, an individual shall be treated as using property as such individual's principal residence during any period of ownership while such individual's spouse or former spouse is granted use of the property under a divorce or separation instrument (as defined in section 71(b)(2)).

"(4) TENANT-STOCKHOLDER IN COOPERATIVE HOUSING CORPORATION. — For purposes of this section, if the taxpayer holds stock as a tenant-stockholder (as defined in section 216) in a cooperative housing corporation (as defined in such section), then—

"(A) the holding requirements of subsection (a) shall be applied to the holding of such stock, and

"(B) the use requirements of subsection (a) shall be applied to the house or apartment which the taxpayer was entitled to occupy as such stockholder.

"(5) INVOLUNTARY CONVERSIONS. —

"(A) IN GENERAL. — For purposes of this section, the destruction, theft, seizure, requisition, or condemnation of property shall be treated as the sale of such property.

"(B) APPLICATION OF SECTION 1033. — In applying section 1033 (relating to involuntary conversions), the amount realized from the sale or exchange of property shall be treated as being the amount determined without regard to this section, reduced by the amount of gain not included in gross income pursuant to this section.

"(C) PROPERTY ACQUIRED AFTER INVOLUNTARY CONVERSION. — If the basis of the property sold or exchanged is determined (in whole or in part) under section 1033(b) (relating to basis of property acquired through involuntary conversion), then the holding and use by the taxpayer of the converted property shall be treated as holding and use by the taxpayer of the property sold or exchanged.

"(6) RECOGNITION OF GAIN ATTRIBUTABLE TO DEPRECIATION.—Subsection (a) shall not apply to so much of the gain from the sale of any property as does not exceed the portion of the depreciation adjustments (as defined in section 1250(b)(3)) attributable to periods after May 6, 1997, in respect of such property.

"(7) DETERMINATION OF USE DURING PERIODS OF OUT-OF-RESIDENCE CARE.—In the case of a taxpayer who—

"(A) becomes physically or mentally incapable of self-care, and

"(B) owns property and uses such property as the taxpayer's principal residence during the 5-year period described in subsection (a) for periods aggregating at least 1 year, then the taxpayer shall be treated as using such property as the taxpayer's principal residence during any time during such 5-year period in which the taxpayer owns the property and resides in any facility (including a nursing home) licensed by a State or political subdivision to care for an individual in the taxpayer's condition.

"(8) SALES OF REMAINDER INTERESTS.—For purposes of this section—

"(A) IN GENERAL.—At the election of the taxpayer, this section shall not fail to apply to the sale or exchange of an interest in a principal residence by reason of such interest being a remainder interest in such residence, but this section shall not apply to any other interest in such residence which is sold or exchanged separately.

"(B) EXCEPTION FOR SALES TO RELATED PARTIES.—Subparagraph (A) shall not apply to any sale to, or exchange with, any person who bears a relationship to the taxpayer which is described in section 267(b) or 707(b).

"(e) DENIAL OF EXCLUSION FOR EXPATRIATES.—This section shall not apply to any sale or exchange by an individual if the treatment provided by section 877(a)(1) applies to such individual.

"(f) ELECTION TO HAVE SECTION NOT APPLY.—This section shall not apply to any sale or exchange with respect to which the taxpayer elects not to have this section apply.

"(g) RESIDENCES ACQUIRED IN ROLLOVERS UNDER SECTION 1034.—For purposes of this section, in the case of property the acquisition of which by the taxpayer resulted under section 1034 (as in effect on the day before the date of the enactment of this section) in the nonrecognition of any part of the gain realized on the sale or exchange of another residence, in determining the period for which the taxpayer has owned and used such property as the taxpayer's principal residence, there shall be included the aggregate periods for which such other residence (and each prior residence taken into account under section 1223(7) in determining the holding period of such property) had been so owned and used.".

(b) REPEAL OF NONRECOGNITION OF GAIN ON ROLLOVER OF PRINCIPAL RESIDENCE.—Section 1034 (relating to rollover of gain on sale of principal residence) is hereby repealed.

(c) EXCEPTION FROM REPORTING.—Subsection (e) of section 6045 (relating to return required in the case of real estate transactions) is amended by adding at the end the following new paragraph:

"(5) EXCEPTION FOR SALES OR EXCHANGES OF CERTAIN PRINCIPAL RESIDENCES.—

"(A) IN GENERAL.—Paragraph (1) shall not apply to any sale or exchange of a residence for $250,000 or less if the person referred to in paragraph (2) receives written assurance in a form acceptable to the Secretary from the seller that—

"(i) such residence is the principal residence (within the meaning of section 121) of the seller,

"(ii) if the Secretary requires the inclusion on the return under subsection (a) of information as to whether there is federally subsidized mortgage financing assistance with respect to the mortgage on residences, that there is no such assistance with respect to the mortgage on such residence, and

"(iii) the full amount of the gain on such sale or exchange is excludable from gross income under section 121.

If such assurance includes an assurance that the seller is married, the preceding sentence shall be applied by substituting '$500,000' for '$250,000'.

The Secretary may by regulation increase the dollar amounts under this subparagraph if the Secretary determines that such an increase will not materially reduce revenues to the Treasury.

"(B) SELLER. — For purposes of this paragraph, the term 'seller' includes the person relinquishing the residence in an exchange.".

(d) CONFORMING AMENDMENTS. —

(1) The following provisions of the Internal Revenue Code of 1986 are each amended by striking "section 1034" and inserting "section 121": sections 25(e)(7), 56(e)(1)(A), 56(e)(3)(B)(i), 143(i)(1)(C)(i)(I), 163(h)(4)(A)(i)(I), 280A(d)(4)(A), 464(f)(3)(B)(i), 1033(h)(4), 1274(c)(3)(B), 6334(a)(13), and 7872(f)(11)(A).

(2) Paragraph (4) of section 32(c) is amended by striking "(as defined in section 1034(h)(3))" and by adding at the end the following new sentence: "For purposes of the preceding sentence, the term 'extended active duty' means any period of active duty pursuant to a call or order to such

duty for a period in excess of 90 days or for an indefinite period.".

(3) Subparagraph (A) of 143(m)(6) is amended by inserting "(as in effect on the day before the date of the enactment of the Taxpayer Relief Act of 1997)" after "1034(e)".

(4) Subsection (e) of section 216 is amended by striking "such exchange qualifies for nonrecognition of gain under section 1034(f)" and inserting "such dwelling unit is used as his principal residence (within the meaning of section 121)".

(5) Section 512(a)(3)(D) is amended by inserting "(as in effect on the day before the date of the enactment of the Taxpayer Relief Act of 1997)" after "1034".

(6) Paragraph (7) of section 1016(a) is amended by inserting "(as in effect on the day before the date of the enactment of the Taxpayer Relief Act of 1997)" after "1034" and by inserting "(as so in effect)" after "1034(e)".

(7) Paragraph (3) of section 1033(k) is amended to read as follows:

"(3) For exclusion from gross income of gain from involuntary conversion of principal residence, see section 121.".

(8) Subsection (e) of section 1038 is amended to read as follows:

"(e) PRINCIPAL RESIDENCES. — If—

"(1) subsection (a) applies to a reacquisition of real property with respect to the sale of which gain was not recognized under section 121 (relating to gain on sale of principal residence); and

"(2) within 1 year after the date of the reacquisition of such property by the seller, such property is resold by him, then, under regulations prescribed by the Secretary, subsections (b), (c), and (d) of this section shall not apply to the reacquisition of such property and, for purposes of applying section 121, the resale of such property shall be treated as a part of the transaction constituting the original sale of such property.".

(9) Paragraph (7) of section 1223 is amended by inserting "(as in effect on the day before the date of the enactment of the Taxpayer Relief Act of 1997)" after "1034".

(10)(A) Subsection (d) of section 1250 is amended by striking paragraph (7) and by redesignating paragraphs (9) and (10) as paragraphs (7) and (8), respectively.

(B) Subsection (e) of section 1250 is amended by striking paragraph (3).

(11) Subsection (c) of section 6012 is amended by striking "(relating to one-time exclusion of gain from sale of principal residence by individual who has attained age 55)" and inserting "(relating to gain from sale of principal residence)".

(12) Paragraph (2) of section 6212(c) is amended by striking subparagraph (C) and by redesignating the succeeding subparagraphs accordingly.

(13) Section 6504 is amended by striking paragraph (4) and by redesignating the succeeding paragraphs accordingly.

(14) The item relating to section 121 in the table of sections for part III of subchapter B of chapter 1 is amended to read as follows:

"Sec. 121. Exclusion of gain from sale of principal residence.".

(15) The table of sections for part III of subchapter O of chapter 1 is amended by striking the item relating to section 1034.

(d) EFFECTIVE DATE. —

(1) IN GENERAL. — The amendments made by this section shall apply to sales and exchanges after May 6, 1997.

(2) SALES BEFORE DATE OF ENACTMENT. — At the election of the taxpayer, the amendments made by this section shall not apply to any sale or exchange before the date of the enactment of this Act.

(3) CERTAIN SALES WITHIN 2 YEARS AFTER DATE OF ENACTMENT. — Section 121 of the Internal Revenue Code of 1986 (as amended by this section) shall be applied without regard to subsection (c)(2)(B) thereof in the case of any sale or exchange of property during the 2-year period beginning on the date of the enactment of this Act if the taxpayer held such property on the date of the enactment of this Act and fails to meet the ownership and use requirements of subsection (a) thereof with respect to such property.

(4) BINDING CONTRACTS. — At the election of the taxpayer, the amendments made by this section shall not apply to a sale or exchange after the date of the enactment of this Act, if—

(A) such sale or exchange is pursuant to a contract which was binding on such date, or

(B) without regard to such amendments, gain would not be recognized under section 1034 of the Internal Revenue Code of 1986 (as in effect on the day before the date of the enactment of this Act) on such sale or exchange by reason of a new residence acquired on or before such date or with respect to the acquisition of which by the taxpayer a binding contract was in effect on such date.

This paragraph shall not apply to any sale or exchange by an individual if the treatment provided by section 877(a)(1) of the Internal Revenue Code of 1986 applies to such individual.

SEC. 313. ROLLOVER OF GAIN FROM SALE OF QUALIFIED STOCK.

(a) IN GENERAL.—Part III of subchapter O of chapter 1 is amended by adding at the end the following new section:

"SEC. 1045. ROLLOVER OF GAIN FROM QUALIFIED SMALL BUSINESS STOCK TO ANOTHER QUALIFIED SMALL BUSINESS STOCK.

"(a) NONRECOGNITION OF GAIN.—In the case of any sale of qualified small business stock held by an individual for more than 6 months and with respect to which such individual elects the application of this section, gain from such sale shall be recognized only to the extent that the amount realized on such sale exceeds—

"(1) the cost of any qualified small business stock purchased by the taxpayer during the 60-day period beginning on the date of such sale, reduced by

"(2) any portion of such cost previously taken into account under this section.

This section shall not apply to any gain which is treated as ordinary income for purposes of this title.

"(b) DEFINITIONS AND SPECIAL RULES.—For purposes of this section—

"(1) QUALIFIED SMALL BUSINESS STOCK.—The term 'qualified small business stock' has the meaning given such term by section 1202(c).

"(2) PURCHASE.—A taxpayer shall be treated as having purchased any property if, but for paragraph (3), the unadjusted basis of such property in the hands of the taxpayer would be its cost (within the meaning of section 1012).

"(3) BASIS ADJUSTMENTS.—If gain from any sale is not recognized by reason of subsection (a), such gain shall be applied to reduce (in the order acquired) the basis for determining gain or loss of any qualified small business stock which is purchased by the taxpayer during the 60-day period described in subsection (a).

"(4) HOLDING PERIOD.—For purposes of determining whether the nonrecognition of gain under subsection (a) applies to stock which is sold—

"(A) the taxpayer's holding period for such stock and the stock referred to in subsection (a)(1) shall be determined without regard to section 1223, and

"(B) only the first 6 months of the taxpayer's holding period for the stock referred to in subsection (a)(1) shall be taken into account for purposes of applying section 1202(c)(2).".

(b) CONFORMING AMENDMENTS.—

(1) Section 1016(a)(23) is amended—

(A) by striking "or 1044" and inserting ", 1044, or 1045", and

(B) by striking "or 1044(d)" and inserting ", 1044(d), or 1045(b)(4)".

(2) Section 1223 is amended by redesignating paragraph (15) as paragraph (16) and by inserting after paragraph (14) the following new paragraph:

"(15) In determining the period for which the taxpayer has held property the acquisition of which resulted under section 1045 in the nonrecognition of any part of the gain realized on the sale of other property, there shall be included the period for which such other property has been held as of the date of such sale.".

(3) The table of sections for part III of subchapter O of chapter 1 is amended by adding at the end the following new item:

"Sec. 1045. Rollover of gain from qualified small business stock to another qualified small business stock.".

(c) EFFECTIVE DATE.—The amendments made by this section shall apply to sales after the date of enactment of this Act.

SEC. 314. AMOUNT OF NET CAPITAL GAIN TAKEN INTO ACCOUNT IN COMPUTING ALTERNATIVE TAX ON CAPITAL GAINS FOR CORPORATIONS NOT TO EXCEED TAXABLE INCOME OF THE CORPORATION.

(a) IN GENERAL.—Paragraph (2) of section 1201(a) is amended by inserting before the period "(or, if less, taxable income)".

(b) EFFECTIVE DATE.—The amendment made by this section shall apply to taxable years ending after December 31, 1997.

APPENDIX B

—▪▪—

The Inflation Factor

WHEN IS A capital gain not a gain?

The answer? When it's only a reflection of inflation.

It's important to understand that in real estate, what is called capital gain is often actually a loss in the purchasing power of money, or, as it's more commonly known, inflation. That doesn't mean, unfortunately, that gain in real estate due to inflation is taxed any less or any differently than gain due to an actual appreciation in the value of the property.

The tax bill proposed in 1995 originally contained several proposals for indexing capital gains—that is, any gain that you made that was due to inflation would not be taxed. This was again proposed for the tax relief bill that eventually passed in 1997. However, none of these proposals made it into the final version of either bill.

That doesn't mean, however, that indexing won't be instituted as part of yet another new tax law in the very near future. Further, if you own real property, it's important that you understand just how much of your gain is real and how much is fantasy, even if you have to pay taxes on all of it.

Understanding your true gain is the only way to make an intelligent decision about whether or not to sell and pay a capital gains tax.

What Is Inflation?

Mark Twain said that the trouble with the weather is that everybody talks about it, but nobody does anything about it. Something similar can be said for inflation. Everybody talks about inflation, but relatively few people understand it well enough to make a calculation based on it.

We all see inflation every day. The price of food, clothing, gasoline, and even housing goes up and up. Back in the late 1970s, the increase reached double-digit levels. In this decade, however, inflation has been moderate, averaging under 4 percent.

:: ALERT! ::

Don't let the low rate fool you. Even at 4 percent a year, the price of everything will double in just 18 years due to inflation alone!

For most of us, inflation is only tangible when the price of something we buy regularly moves up a notch. For example, We've been buying hardcover books at our local bookstore for a top price of $19.95. Now that top price has moved up to $24.95.

Or, we've purchased shirts regularly for $20 to $25. Now shirts cost $30 to $45.

Or, we buy a new car every five years. The car we bought last time cost around $17,000. Today, a similar car with no real improvements costs over $20,000.

Everywhere we look, prices go up, and for most of us, that's what inflation means. But inflation isn't the increase in price—that's just the symptom. Inflation means the decrease in buying power of our money. When the dollar buys less, the symptom is higher prices across the board.

There are two major indexes of inflation.

- The consumer price index (CPI) measures inflation by the increase in price of a select group of consumer items including food, housing, clothing, and so on.

- The wholesale price index (WPI) measures inflation by the increase in prices of goods at the wholesale level. It is considered a better indicator of future inflation, since it takes time for the effects of wholesale prices to work their way down to the retail level.

When the government says that inflation is moving along at, for example, 4 percent a year, what is really being referred to is the CPI (or, less frequently, the WPI). The CPI is going up at that rate. Or, to put it in more technically accurate terms, our money is losing about 4 percent a year in value—in purchasing power.

How Does Inflation Influence Real Estate Values?

Real estate is a commodity just like shirts, books, and cars. If we assume for a moment that a piece of property has a constant value and if we acknowledge that our money is worth less today than it was yesterday, then the price for the property will inevitably go up. (There are some problems with out first assumption; we'll deal with those shortly.)

- We bought a piece of real estate three years ago for $100,000. Today it's worth $112,000. How much did the property truly appreciate in price and how much did it go up simply due to inflation?

- Let's calculate this using our fingers and toes. (Yes, it's easier to use a formula, but this way makes it much clearer.) We'll assume an annual inflation rate of just 3 percent.

Year one:	Value	$100,000
	Inflation	×3%
	Increase to	$103,000
Year two:	Value	$103,000
	Inflation	×3%
	Increase to	$106,090
Year three:	Value	$106,090
	Inflation	×3%
	Increase to	$110,107

How Much of My Capital Gain Is Due to Inflation?

If our property (in the above example) is worth $112,000 after three years, then a little more than $10,000 of that perceived increase in property value is actually a decrease in money value—inflation. Our true appreciation is only about $2000!

Common sense dictates that we should only have to pay capital gains tax when our capital appreciates in value—when our property becomes worth more. This occurs because we've improved the property or because some external influence such as rezoning, the arrival of better transportation, or the building of a new mall or more expensive nearby housing has increased its value.

We should not have to pay tax on the loss of value of our money. However, in fact there is currently no distinction made between a gain due to inflation and a gain due to true property value appreciation. A capital gains tax is due on both.

How Do I Calculate My True Capital Gain?

If you're considering selling your property and taking out your profits, it would behoove you to know your true capital gain.

The reason is that you want to know whether you have a true capital gain or simply an illusory inflation-induced gain. The last thing you want to do is sell for an inflationary gain and then pay capital gains taxes on the sale. In essence, you would be paying the government a tax on the loss of value of your own money! You could end up with a loss in your pocket after taxes and think it was a gain.

:: TAX TRAVAIL ::

Unfortunately, this is exactly what a great many real estate investors have done and continue to do. Of course, the new reduced capital gains tax rate means the amount you're paying in taxes is less. But any taxes paid on an inflation-caused increase in value seem to be questionable. The savvy seller first determines just how much his or her property has truly increased in value before making the selling decision.

If you're not sure how this all works, let's take an example.

- In our earlier example, there was an increase of roughly $10,000 in property value due to inflation alone. Let's assume that the entire inflation-caused "profit" could be taken out on the sale (no closing costs). Would that gain be taxable? If it were a capital gain, indeed it would. Remember, the government doesn't currently distinguish between a true capital gain and an inflationary gain. In the 28 percent tax bracket, the tax would be $2000.

If your entire "profit" is caused by inflation, that means that your property really didn't appreciate in value. Thus, if you sell and take out that inflationary profit, you end up paying tax on, in essence, nothing. You'd be paying the tax out of your own pocket!

How Do I Make the Selling Decision?

A savvy seller will first determine which portion of gain on the property is due to inflation and which is due to true appreciation. To do this, you must first determine the inflation rate during the time you owned the property and then subtract that from your actual capital gain.

- In our above example, the gain due to inflation was roughly $10,000. What if the total capital gain on which taxes were paid was $20,000? You would pay tax on $20,000, assuming at a 20 percent rate, for a total of $4,000.

- However, because only half of the capital gain was due to true appreciation of the property, the actual level of taxation would be 40 percent. Because of the inflation factor, you'd actually be paying twice the listed rate!

- In the same example, what if your total gain was $40,000 and the inflation portion of it was still $10,000? How much tax would you pay now? You would pay tax on the entire $40,000 (assuming you were in the 28 percent or higher tax bracket). Your tax would be roughly $8000.

- However, because only three-fourths of the capital gain was due to true appreciation of the property, the actual level of taxation would be about 25 percent. Because of the inflation factor, again you'd actually be paying more than the listed tax rate.

- Because inflation is not taken out of the calculation for capital gain, it increases the amount of tax that you are really paying. You may think you're only paying 20 percent (effective) in capital gains taxes. But with inflation added in, you could be paying much, much more.

What you must decide is, When does the capital gain reach high enough levels to outweigh the monetary loss due to inflation?

Under the old capital gains system of up to 28 percent, the hit that you took would be much stiffer. Under the new reduced capital gains rate, the cost is much less. But there is still a cost.

✄ TAX HINT ✄

Always remember that whenever you are quoted a tax rate for a capital gain (including elsewhere in this book), the rate being quoted does not take inflation into account. If you take inflation into account, your true capital appreciation is much smaller and your true capital gains tax rate is much higher.

You may reverse your decision to sell when you are confronted by the true figures. Indeed, you may wish to hang onto the property for a longer period of time or do a "tax-free" trade (1031). In some cases, you may wish you had never purchased the property in the first place! Of course, with prices generally on the upswing, real profits may once again soon return and big capital gains may warrant paying the hidden inflation tax.

Index

—◼◼—

A

Accelerated depreciation, vs. straight-line depreciation, 95–96
Active/passive rules, effect of, on depreciation, 100–101
Alternative minimum tax (AMT), 39, 100

B

Basis
    change of, 78
    definition of, 75
    effects of gift/inheritance on calculation of, 87–88
    example calculations of, 75, 76, 77–78
    methods of lowering, 79–81
        examples of calculation, 80–85
    purchase expenses and, 75–76
    and refinancing of property, 85–87
    typical property improvements leading to increase in, 78–79
    when building a home, 77–78

"Boot" (cash), of trade transactions, 110, 112
Bullion, treatment/inclusion of, in IRAs, 156–159
Buy and hold for a long time strategy, 129–132
Buy/sell strategies, in capital gains tax reduction
    buy and hold for a long time strategy, 129–132
    conversion strategy, 125–129
    fix-up strategy, 135–136
    good timing strategy, 132–134
    serial purchase/sale strategy, 129

C

Capital
    definition/nature of, 4–5
    high rate of taxation on, in United States, 4
    risking of, as essential to society, 5
    as stored product of work, 4
    taxation of, as anticapitalist, 6
Capital gains tax
    argument for elimination of, 5–6